COMPUTER SCIENCE, TECHNOLOGY AND APPLICATIONS

SOFT COMPUTING

DEVELOPMENTS, METHODS AND APPLICATIONS

COMPUTER SCIENCE, TECHNOLOGY AND APPLICATIONS

Additional books in this series can be found on Nova's website under the Series tab.

Additional e-books in this series can be found on Nova's website under the eBooks tab.

COMPUTER SCIENCE, TECHNOLOGY AND APPLICATIONS

SOFT COMPUTING

DEVELOPMENTS, METHODS AND APPLICATIONS

ALAN CASEY
EDITOR

nova publishers
New York

Library of Congress Cataloging-in-Publication Data

Names: Casey, Alan, editor.
Title: Soft computing : developments, methods and applications / [edited by] Alan Casey.
Other titles: Soft computing (Casey)
Description: Hauppauge, New York : Nova Science Publishers, Inc., [2016] | Series: Computer science, technology and applications | Includes bibliographical references and index. | Description based on print version record and CIP data provided by publisher; resource not viewed.
Identifiers: LCCN 2016017653 (print) | LCCN 2016014503 (ebook) | ISBN 9781634851510 () | ISBN 9781634851336 (hardcover)
Subjects: LCSH: Soft computing.
Classification: LCC QA76.9.S63 (print) | LCC QA76.9.S63 S578 2016 (ebook) | DDC 006.3--dc23
LC record available at https://lccn.loc.gov/2016017653

Published by Nova Science Publishers, Inc. † New York

CONTENTS

PREFACE

This book discusses developments, methods and applications of soft computing. Chapter One depicts the increasing efficiency of the soft computing algorithms and fuzzy information processing models by developing a library of universal analytic models for fuzzy arithmetic operations with asymmetrical triangular fuzzy numbers (TrFNs). Chapter Two examines the determination of stability number of layered slope using Adaptive Neuro-Fuzzy Inference System (ANFIS), Gaussian Process Regression (GPR), Relevance Vector Machine (RVM), Extreme Learning Machine (ELM). Chapter Three discusses the intensive developing of Soft Computing systems especially Wavelet-Neuro-Fuzzy Systems (WNFS) in Dynamic Data Mining tasks, when the data are fed sequentially to the processing in on-line mode.

In: Soft Computing
Editor: Alan Casey

ISBN: 978-1-63485-133-6

Chapter 1

REDUCED LIBRARY OF THE SOFT COMPUTING ANALYTIC MODELS FOR ARITHMETIC OPERATIONS WITH ASYMMETRICAL FUZZY NUMBERS

***Yuriy P. Kondratenko*[1,2,*] *and Nina Y. Kondratenko*[3,†]**
[1]Department of Electrical Engineering and Computer Science
Washkewicz College of Engineering, Cleveland State University, Cleveland, OH, US
[2]Department of Intelligent Information Systems
Petro Mohyla Black Sea State University, Mykolaiv, Ukraine
[3]Darla Moore School of Business, University of South Carolina, Columbia, SC, US

ABSTRACT

This chapter depicts the increasing efficiency of the soft computing algorithms and fuzzy information processing models by developing a Library of universal analytic models for fuzzy arithmetic operations with asymmetrical triangular fuzzy numbers (TrFNs). Special attention is paid to the arithmetic operations "addition" and "subtraction" and their

* Corresponding Author address – Prof. Dr.Sc. Yuriy P. Kondratenko.
Email: y.kondratenko@csuohio.edu, y_kondrat2002@yahoo.com.
† E-mail: nykondratenko@gmail.com.

peculiarities in the cases of TrFNs with different shapes of the resulting membership functions. Authors present reduced Library of the inverse and direct analytic models of the result's MFs with the detailed description of the proposed reducing procedure. The chapter also covers the application of the modeling results and specific properties of the soft computing models' Library to solving of the real-life optimization problems in uncertainty.

Keywords: soft computing, asymmetrical triangular fuzzy number, fuzzy arithmetic, resulting model's library, inverse model, direct model

1. INTRODUCTION

For mathematical formalization of uncertain processes and control or decision-making systems, which are functioning in uncertainty, it is feasible to use the theory of fuzzy sets [29, 30, 44, 45]. First article on "fuzzy sets" was published fifty years ago by L. Zadeh [44] and there are many important theoretical contributions to the developments of fuzzy sets and fuzzy logic theory made by scientists all over the world [11, 12, 22, 25, 28, 35, 36, 37]. The acknowledgement of fuzzy sets theory in academic world is related to the wide practical applications of its mathematical methods in different areas [8, 9, 10, 14, 22, 40, 45]: technical diagnostics, medicine, transportation science, computer science, business process management, engineering, economics, finances and others.

The membership function (MF) [13, 29, 33, 44] that exists in the interval [0, 1] is the main characteristic of any fuzzy set. Let us consider a fuzzy set $\underset{\sim}{A}$ that is specified on the universal set E. In this case, any element x of the fuzzy set $\underset{\sim}{A}$ corresponds to a specific value of the membership function (MF) $\mu_{\underset{\sim}{A}}(x) \in [0,1]$. Thus, fuzzy set $\underset{\sim}{A}$ is called [29],[33],[44] the set of pairs

$$\left(x, \mu_{\underset{\sim}{A}}(x)\right),$$

where $x \in E,\ \mu_{\underset{\sim}{A}}(x) \in [0,1]$.

Special attention needs to be devoted to the fuzzy arithmetic that considers the rules, properties, algorithms and mathematical models for implementation of various arithmetic operations$(*)$, including addition, subtraction, multiplication and division, $(*) \in \{(+),(-),(\times),(:)\}$. The efficiency of the arithmetic operations depends on the accuracy of calculations, calculation time, and algorithm complexity and so on. Fuzzy sets which are normal and convex are referred to as fuzzy numbers [13, 29, 33]. For the presentation of the various kinds of uncertain information in granular or fuzzy style it is possible to use different fuzzy numbers (FN) with different shapes of membership functions. Among them are MFs [13, 29, 35]: Gaussian symmetrical function, Gaussian asymmetrical function, sigmoid function, internal and external (left, right) harmonic functions, polynomial (second order and high order) MFs and others. Membership functions with straight segments (left outside, right outside, trapezoidal, rectangular, triangular) are very convenient for the evaluation of the uncertain data by the qualified experts. Most popular among them are the fuzzy numbers with triangular shapes of membership function (TrFN). The implementation of fuzzy arithmetic operations for triangular fuzzy numbers is covered in several prior publications [13, 38, 43]. Special attention is paid to the development of universal direct and inverse models for the resulting fuzzy sets obtained as a result of fuzzy information processing based on the implementation of fuzzy arithmetic operations [7, 13, 15, 16, 17, 18, 20]. It is common to adapt such universal resulting models to the different shapes of TrFN, for example, for the TrFN with different asymmetrical shapes of the membership functions. In [19] authors consider the library of universal models consisting of 16 different resulting fuzzy models for all possible combinations of the symmetrical and asymmetrical TrFNs. At the same time the optimization of the library's size by reducing the number of the resulting universal models is a very important task for the decreasing calculation complexity and time, taking into account the specific characteristics of the concrete arithmetic operations and their resulting analytic models.

The aim of this chapter is to propose an optimisation of the library by decreasing the number of analytical models of the resulting MFs, in particular, for arithmetic operation "addition" and "subtraction" with any combinations of symmetrical and asymmetrical TrFNs, providing an opportunity for reducing the volume and complexity, improving their operating speed as well as increasing the accuracy of the fuzzy information processing in computerized control and decision support systems [5, 6, 11, 28, 43]. Section 2 provides an insight to the analysis of the inverse and direct models of the resulting MFs for fuzzy arithmetic with triangular fuzzy numbers. Section 3 covers the mask's representation of the TrFNs with varios shapes of MFs. In Section 4 authors describe the peculiarities of the asymmetrical TrFNs' combinations based on the examples of the fuzzy arithmetic operations. Section 5 represents the reduced Library of inverse and direct models for realization of arithmetic operations "addition" and "subtraction" with asymmetrical TrFNs. Finally, the applied directions for implementation of the reduced Library of the resulting fuzzy analytic models are discussed in Section 6. The chapter ends with a conclusion in Section 7 and an acknowledgment in Section 8.

2. Analysis of the Inverse and Direct Models of the TrFNs

The analytic model for the membership function $\mu_{\underset{\sim}{A}}(x)$ of the fuzzy set $\underset{\sim}{A}$ is a direct (vertical) model [13, 33], which provides the possibilities to calculate the value of membership grade $\mu_{\underset{\sim}{A}}(\cdot)$ for any value of x, included to support the fuzzy set $\underset{\sim}{A}$:

$$\forall x : x \in S(\underset{\sim}{A}) = \text{supp}(\underset{\sim}{A}) = \{x : \mu_{\underset{\sim}{A}}(x) > 0, x \in E\}.$$

The inverse (horizontal) model [13, 29] of the fuzzy set $\underset{\sim}{A}$ can be presented as crisp α-level set A_α as follows:

$$A_\alpha = \{x | \mu_{\underset{\sim}{A}}(x) \geq \alpha\},\ \alpha \in [0,1].$$

In general, α- cuts of the fuzzy set $\underset{\sim}{A} \in R$ is an ordinary (in terms of conditions $\mu_{\underset{\sim}{A}}(x) \geq \alpha$) subset that contains elements $x \in R$ with fuzzy set degree of membership $\underset{\sim}{A}$ not less than value α.

It is possible to use the inverse analytic models for implementation of the arithmetic operations, but computational algorithms based on the α-cuts of the relevant fuzzy sets [15, 17, 18, 19] have a high computational complexity, as it is performed in turn for all α - levels:

$$\alpha_{i+1} = \alpha_i + \Delta\alpha,\ (\alpha_i \in [0,\ 1],\ \ i = 0, 1, 2, ..., r,\ \alpha_0 = 0,\ \alpha_r = 1)$$

with the step of discreteness $\Delta\alpha$. The value of $\Delta\alpha$ significantly affects the accuracy and operating speed of the computational procedures performance [15, 18, 19].

Thus, the using of the corresponding analytic models based on the generalized direct approach allows formalizing the procedures of fuzzy arithmetic operations and improving such parameters as dependability, operating speed and accuracy of their realizations [14, 16, 17, 19].

If the fuzzy number $\underset{\sim}{A}$ has the triangular's shape of MF $\mu_{\underset{\sim}{A}}(x)$, then this FN is called the triangular fuzzy number TrFN, which can be presented in the special mathematical form [13, 29, 33]:

$$\underset{\sim}{A} = (a_1, a_0, a_2),$$

where $\mu_{\underset{\sim}{A}}(a_1) = 0;\ \mu_{\underset{\sim}{A}}(a_0) = 1;\ \ \mu_{\underset{\sim}{A}}(a_2) = 0$.

Inverse models A_α and B_α of the corresponding TrFNs $\underset{\sim}{A}$ and $\underset{\sim}{B}$ and their direct models in the triangular form $\mu_{\underset{\sim}{A}}(x)$ and $\mu_{\underset{\sim}{B}}(x)$ are determined [13, 16, 19] by the appropriate relevant dependencies (1), (2) and (3), (4):

$$A_\alpha = [a_1(\alpha),\ a_2(\alpha)] = [a_1 + \alpha(a_0 - a_1),\ a_2 - \alpha(a_2 - a_0)\ ], \tag{1}$$

$$B_\alpha = [b_1(\alpha),\ b_2(\alpha)] = [b_1 + \alpha(b_0 - b_1),\ b_2 - \alpha(b_2 - b_0)\ ], \tag{2}$$

$$\mu_{\underset{\sim}{A}}(x) = \begin{cases} 0, \forall (x \le a_1) \cup (x \ge a_2) \\ (x - a_1)/(a_0 - a_1), \forall (a_1 < x \le a_0) \\ (a_2 - x)/(a_2 - a_0), \forall (a_0 < x < a_2) \end{cases}. \tag{3}$$

$$\mu_{\underset{\sim}{B}}(x) = \begin{cases} 0, \forall (x \le b_1) \cup (x \ge b_2) \\ (x - b_1)/(b_0 - b_1), \forall (b_1 < x \le b_0) \\ (b_2 - x)/(b_2 - b_0), \forall (b_0 < x < b_2) \end{cases}. \tag{4}$$

Crisp sets $A_\alpha = [a_1(\alpha),\ a_2(\alpha)]$ and $B_\alpha = [b_1(\alpha),\ b_2(\alpha)]$ determine the appropriate α-cuts of the fuzzy sets $\underset{\sim}{A}$ and $\underset{\sim}{B}$, where $\alpha \in [0,\ 1]$, $\underset{\sim}{A}, \underset{\sim}{B} \in R^+$, and resulting inverse models C_α for the arithmetic operations "addition" and "subtraction" can be written as [13, 16, 19, 29, 33, 43]:

$$C_\alpha = A_\alpha(+)B_\alpha = [a_1(\alpha),\ a_2(\alpha)](+)[b_1(\alpha),\ b_2(\alpha)] = \\ = [a_1(\alpha)+b_1(\alpha),\ a_2(\alpha)+b_2(\alpha)], \tag{5}$$

$$C_\alpha = A_\alpha(-)B_\alpha = [a_1(\alpha), a_2(\alpha)](-)[b_1(\alpha), b_2(\alpha)] = \\ = [a_1(\alpha)-b_2(\alpha),\ a_2(\alpha)-b_1(\alpha)]. \tag{6}$$

Direct analytic model $\mu_{\underset{\sim}{C}}(x)$ of the resulting MF, synthesized using [13, 16, 18, 29, 33], can be presented for the arithmetic operation of addition $\underset{\sim}{C} = \underset{\sim}{A}(+)\underset{\sim}{B}$ as follows:

$$\forall x \in R:$$

$$\mu_{\underset{\sim}{C}}(x) = \begin{cases} 0, & \forall(x \le a_1 + b_1) \cup (x \ge a_2 + b_2) \\ (x - a_1 - b_1)/(a_0 + b_0 - a_1 - b_1), & \forall(a_1 + b_1 < x \le a_0 + b_0) \\ (a_2 + b_2 - x)/(a_2 + b_2 - a_0 - b_0), & \forall(a_0 + b_0 < x < a_2 + b_2) \end{cases}. \tag{7}$$

Direct analytic model $\mu_{\underset{\sim}{C}}(x)$ of the resulting MF, synthesized using [13, 16, 18, 33], can be presented for the arithmetic operation of subtraction $\underset{\sim}{C} = \underset{\sim}{A}(-)\underset{\sim}{B}$ as follows:

$$\forall x \in R:$$

$$\mu_{\underset{\sim}{C}}(x) = \begin{cases} 0, & \forall(x \le a_1 - b_2) \cup (x \ge a_2 - b_1) \\ (x - a_1 + b_2)/(a_0 + b_2 - a_1 - b_0), & \forall(a_1 - b_2 < x \le a_0 - b_0) \\ (a_2 - b_1 - x)/(a_2 + b_0 - a_0 - b_1), & \forall(a_0 - b_0 < x < a_2 - b_1) \end{cases}. \tag{8}$$

3. The Boolean Masks for the Representations of TrFNs with Various Shapes

The direct models $\mu_{\underset{\sim}{C}}(x)$, represented in equations (7) and (8) for arithmetic operation "addition" and "subtraction," are validated [19, 20] for the symmetrical TrFNs $\underset{\sim}{A}=(a_1,a_0,a_2)$ and $\underset{\sim}{B}=(b_1,b_0,b_2)$ under the following conditions:

$$a_1 < a_0 < a_2,\ b_1 < b_0 < b_2 .$$

At the same time, a lot of the real input values for decision-making processes can be presented as TrFNs with different assymmetrical shapes of the MF and for each concrete case a decision-maker should develop the analytic model of the resulting fuzzy set for implementation of arithmetic operations "addition" and/or "subtraction."

In [19] authors developed a 16-component library of inverse and direct analytic models of the resulting fuzzy set, for example $\tilde{C}$, for realization of the corresponding arithmetic operation "addition" with TrFNs, $\underset{\sim}{A}$ and $\underset{\sim}{B}$, in the set of non-negative real numbers R^+ for various combinations of the MF's shapes (Table 1). The assymetical shapes of the TrFNs can be evaluated using corresponding masks of TrFNs [19, 24]:

$$\text{Mask } (\underset{\sim}{A},\underset{\sim}{B})=\{s,n,m,r\}=\text{Mask } \underset{\sim}{A}=\{s,n\}(\cup)\text{Mask } \underset{\sim}{B}=\{m,r\}, \quad (9)$$

where indicators s,n,m and r can be defined as

$$s=\begin{cases}0, & \text{if } a_0 > a_1 \\ 1, & \text{if } a_0 = a_1\end{cases}; \quad n=\begin{cases}0, & \text{if } a_0 < a_2 \\ 1, & \text{if } a_0 = a_2\end{cases};$$

$$m=\begin{cases}0, & \text{if } b_0 > b_1 \\ 1, & \text{if } b_0 = b_1\end{cases}; \quad r=\begin{cases}0, & \text{if } b_0 < b_2 \\ 1, & \text{if } b_0 = b_2\end{cases}.$$

4. Asymmetrical TrFNs' Combinations and Their Peculiarities in Fuzzy Arithmetic

The procedure of the synthesis of the inverse and direct analytic models consist of several steps [19, 20, 21]. Let us consider, as an example, the main steps of this procedure for arithmetic operation "addition."

Step 1. The formation, based on (5), of the inverse model C_α for $\alpha-$cuts of a fuzzy set $\underset{\sim}{C}=\underset{\sim}{A}(+)\underset{\sim}{B}=(c_1,c_0,c_2)$ as TrFN:

$$C_\alpha = A_\alpha(+)B_\alpha = [a_1(\alpha)+b_1(\alpha),\ a_2(\alpha)+b_2(\alpha)] = [c_1(\alpha), c_2(\alpha)], \tag{10}$$

where $c_1(\alpha)=a_1(\alpha)+b_1(\alpha);$ (11)

$$c_2(\alpha)= a_2(\alpha)+b_2(\alpha). \tag{12}$$

Step 2. The determination, using the corresponding equations (11) and (12), of the parameter α:

(a) for the left branch $c_1(\alpha)$

$$\alpha = f_L\left[c_1(\alpha), a_1, a_0, b_1, b_0\right]$$

and (b) for the right branch $c_2(\alpha)$ of the of the resulting MF $\underset{\sim}{C}=\underset{\sim}{A}(+)\underset{\sim}{B}$:

$$\alpha = f_R\left[c_2(\alpha), a_2, a_0, b_2, b_0\right].$$

Step 3. The transition from inverse to direct approach [13, 15, 16, 19] shows that variable x is a parameter of the functions $\alpha = f_L\left[c_1(\alpha), a_1, a_0, b_1, b_0\right]$ and $\alpha = f_R\left[c_2(\alpha), a_2, a_0, b_2, b_0\right]$, that is

$$\alpha = f_L\left[x, a_1, a_0, b_1, b_0\right] \text{ for } x=c_1(\alpha)\in[c_1,c_0];$$

$$\alpha = f_R\left[x, a_2, a_0, b_2, b_0\right] \text{ for } x=c_2(\alpha)\in[c_0,c_2].$$

Table 1. Masks for combinations of TrFNs and their models

No.	$\underset{\sim}{A}=(a_1,a_0,a_2)$	$\underset{\sim}{B}=(b_1,b_0,b_2)$	$\{s,n,m,r\}$	$\underset{\sim}{C}=\underset{\sim}{A}(\pm)\underset{\sim}{B}$
1	Symmetrical	Symmetrical	$\{0,0,0,0\}$	MM_1
2	Symmetrical	Right asymmetrical	$\{0,0,0,1\}$	MM_2
3	Symmetrical	Left asymmetrical	$\{0,0,1,0\}$	MM_3
4	Symmetrical	Asymmetrical (Left/Right)	$\{0,0,1,1\}$	MM_4
5	Right asymmetrical	Symmetrical	$\{0,1,0,0\}$	MM_5
6	Right asymmetrical	Right asymmetrical	$\{0,1,0,1\}$	MM_6
7	Right asymmetrical	Left asymmetrical	$\{0,1,1,0\}$	MM_7
8	Right asymmetrical	Asymmetrical (Left/Right)	$\{0,1,1,1\}$	MM_8
9	Left asymmetrical	Symmetrical	$\{1,0,0,0\}$	MM_9
10	Left asymmetrical	Right asymmetrical	$\{1,0,0,1\}$	MM_{10}
11	Left asymmetrical	Left asymmetrical	$\{1,0,1,0\}$	MM_{11}
12	Left asymmetrical	Asymmetrical (Left/Right)	$\{1,0,1,1\}$	MM_{12}
13	Asymmetrical (Left/Right)	Symmetrical	$\{1,1,0,0\}$	MM_{13}
14	Asymmetrical (Left/Right)	Right asymmetrical	$\{1,1,0,1\}$	MM_{14}
15	Asymmetrical (Left/Right)	Left asymmetrical	$\{1,1,1,0\}$	MM_{15}
16	Asymmetrical (Left/Right)	Asymmetrical (Left/Right)	$\{1,1,1,1\}$	MM_{16}

Step 4. The formation of the direct analytical model for resulting MF of fuzzy set $\underset{\sim}{C}=\underset{\sim}{A}(+)\underset{\sim}{B}$ by substituting $\mu_{\underset{\sim}{C}}(x)$ instead of α :

$$\mu_{\underset{\sim}{C}}(x)=\begin{cases} 0, & \forall(x\le c_1)\cup(x\ge(c_2)) \\ f_L[x,a_1,a_0,b_1,b_0], & \forall(c_1<x\le c_0) \\ f_R[x,a_2,a_0,b_2,b_0], & \forall(c_0<x\le c_2) \end{cases}. \quad (13)$$

Table 1 presents all possible combinations of TrFNs $(\underset{\sim}{A},\underset{\sim}{B})$, their masks Mask $(\underset{\sim}{A},\underset{\sim}{B})=\{s,n,m,r\}$ for different shapes of MFs and corresponding mathematical models $\{MM_1,MM_2,...,MM_{16}\}$ for realisation of any $(\pm)$ arithmetic operation, $(\pm)\in\{(+),(-)\}$. In [19] the authors represent the inverse and direct models $\{MM_1,MM_2,...,MM_{16}\}$ according to the input data from Table 1, which were synthesized based on the abovementioned 4-steps procedure for different shapes of TrFNs $\underset{\sim}{A}$ and $\underset{\sim}{B}$, using, as an example, the arithmetic operation "addition": $\underset{\sim}{C}=\underset{\sim}{A}(+)\underset{\sim}{B}$. The approach proposed in [19] is efficient for any arithmetic operation, but at the same time, the deep analysis of each concrete arithmetic operation and corresponding resulting inverse and direct models gives possibilities for the reduction of the size of the 16-component (Table 1) library.

Analyzing the resulting direct model (7) for the arithmetic operation "addition" $\underset{\sim}{C}=\underset{\sim}{A}(+)\underset{\sim}{B}$, it is possible to make the conclusions that the direct model (7) should be transformed to the set of corresponding models only for such pairs of the asymmetrical TrFNs with the following parametric conditions:

a) $a_1=a_0,\quad b_1=b_0$ (simultaneously); (14)

b) $a_2=a_0,\quad b_2=b_0$ (simultaneously). (15)

In this case, the reduced Library of resulting models should only consist of the direct and inverse models for the masks:

Mask $(\underset{\sim}{A},\underset{\sim}{B})=\{1,n,1,r\},n=\{0,1\},r=\{0,1\}$;

Mask $\left(\underset{\sim}{A},\underset{\sim}{B}\right)=\{s,1,m,1\},s=\{0,1\},m=\{0,1\}$.

Analyzing the resulting direct model (8) for arithmetic operation "subtraction" $\underset{\sim}{C}=\underset{\sim}{A}(-)\underset{\sim}{B}$, it is possible to make the conclusions that the direct model (8) should be transformed to the set of corresponding models only for such pairs of the asymmetrical TrFNs with the following parametric conditions:

a) $a_1=a_0,\ \ b_2=b_0$ (simultaneously); (16)

b) $a_2=a_0,\ \ b_1=b_0$ (simultaneously). (17)

In this second case, the reduced Library of the resulting models should consist of only the direct and inverse models for the masks:

Mask $\left(\underset{\sim}{A},\underset{\sim}{B}\right)=\{1,n,m,1\},n=\{0,1\},m=\{0,1\}$;

Mask $\left(\underset{\sim}{A},\underset{\sim}{B}\right)=\{s,1,1,r\},s=\{0,1\},r=\{0,1\}$.

5. Reduced Library of Inverse and Direct Models for Arithmetic Operations "Addition" and "Subtraction" with Asymmetrical TrFNs

Figure 1 represents the algorithm for the arithmetic operation "addition" based on the 16-component library MM_1-MM_{16} [19], which was modified to reduced 8-component Library of analytic models $\{MM_1,MM_6,MM_8,MM_{11},MM_{12},MM_{14},MM_{15},MM_{16}\}$ for different shapes of TrFNs $\left(\underset{\sim}{A},\underset{\sim}{B}\right)$.

The main components of the proposed algorithm (Figure 1) are:

- a step-by-step evaluation of the Mask$\{s,n,m,r\}$ for the TrFN's pair $\left(\underset{\sim}{A},\underset{\sim}{B}\right)$ based on the Mask$\{s,n\}$ for TrFN $\underset{\sim}{A}=\left(a_1,a_0,a_2\right)$ and Mask $\{m,r\}$ for TrFN $\underset{\sim}{B}=\left(b_1,b_0,b_2\right)$;

- the choice of the corresponding analytic model MM^* from the reduced set of the models:

$$MM^* \in \left\{MM_{1,+}, MM_{6,+}, MM_{8,+}, MM_{11,+}, MM_{12,+}, MM_{14,+}, MM_{15,+}, MM_{16,+}\right\},$$

where index $(z,+)$ means that mathematical model $MM_{z,+}$ can be used for arithmetic operation "addition";

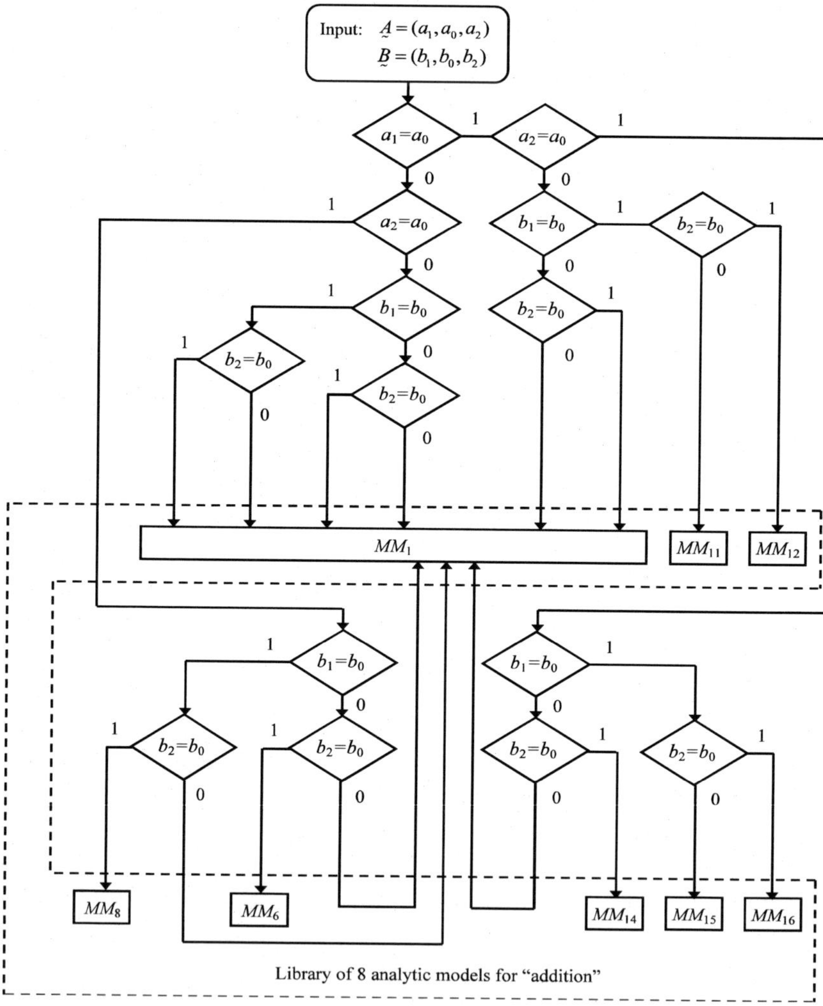

Figure 1. Flowchart for chosing corresponding analytical model according to the masks of TrFNs with different shapes of MFs: arithmetic operation "addition."

$z \in \{1,6,8,11,12,14,15,16\}$.

When analytic model *MM** is chosen (Figure 1), then it is possible:

- to choose the direct model $\mu_{\underset{\sim}{C}}(x)$ of the resulting fuzzy set $\underset{\sim}{C}$;
- to calculate the MF for the resulting fuzzy set $\underset{\sim}{C}$ or the value of MF's grade $\mu_{\underset{\sim}{C}}(x^*)$ for the desired argument x^*, using the direct model $\mu_{\underset{\sim}{C}}(x)$.

For the arithmetic operation "subtraction" it is necessary to choose the corresponding analytic model MM^*, according to Mask$\{s,n,m,r\}$, from the next reduced set of the models:

$$MM^* \in \{MM_{1,-}, MM_{7,-}, MM_{8,-}, MM_{10,-}, MM_{12,-}, MM_{14,-}, MM_{15,-}, MM_{16,-}\},$$

where index $(z,-)$ means that mathematical model $MM_{z,-}$ can be used for arithmetic operation "subtraction";

$z \in \{1,7,8,10,12,14,15,16\}$.

The Perl-pseudo code (m-file) for determination of the masks of TrFNs and corresponding mathematical models $MM_i, i \in \{1,7,8,10,12,14,15,16\}$ from the 8-component Library for fuzzy arithmetic operation "subtraction" can be presented as follows:

```
a1=A(1);a0=A(2);a2=A(3);
b1=B(1);b0=B(2);b2=B(3);
S=0;
if a1==a0
    if a2==a0
        if b1==b0
            if b2==b0
                S=S+1;
                disp('Mask={1,1,1,1} AND model is MM16')
            else S=S+1;
```

```
                disp('Mask={1,1,1,0} AND model is MM15')
            end
        elseif b2==b0
            S=S+1;
                disp('Mask={1,1,0,1} AND model is MM14')
        end
    elseif b1==b0
            if b2==b0
                S=S+1;
            disp('Mask={1,0,1,1} AND model is MM12')
            end
    elseif b2==b0
                S=S+1;
            disp('Mask={1,0,0,1} AND model is MM10')
    end
elseif a2==a0
        if b1==b0
            if b2==b0
                S=S+1;
            disp('Mask={0,1,1,1} AND model is MM8')
            else
                S=S+1;
            disp('Mask={0,1,1,1} AND model is MM7')
            end
        end
end
        if S==0
            disp('S=0 AND model is MM1')
        end
```

The Table 2 consists of the selected inverse models $C_\alpha = A_\alpha(\pm)B_\alpha = [c_1(\alpha), c_2(\alpha)]$ for resulting fuzzy sets, in particular, 8 models $C_\alpha = A_\alpha(+)B_\alpha$ for the arithmetic operation "addition" and 8 models $C_\alpha = A_\alpha(-)B_\alpha$ for the arithmetic operation "subtraction." In general case [19] the library will consists of 32 inverse models (16 models for addition and 16 models for subtraction). According to the authors' proposition (14)-(17), the reduction of the models' number in the modified library is 16 (8 models for

Table 2. Reduced Library of the inverse models for resulting TFN
$\underset{\sim}{C} = \underset{\sim}{A}(\pm)\underset{\sim}{B}$

$MM_{i,+,-}$	$C_\alpha = A_\alpha(\pm)B_\alpha = [c_1(\alpha), c_2(\alpha)]$
$MM_{1,+}$	$[(a_1+b_1)+\alpha((a_0+b_0)-(a_1+b_1)),(a_2+b_2)-\alpha((a_2+b_2)-(a_0+b_0))]$
$MM_{1,-}$	$[(a_1-b_2)+\alpha((a_0+b_2)-(a_1+b_0)),(a_2-b_1)-\alpha((a_2+b_0)-(a_0+b_1))]$
$MM_{6,+}$	$[(a_1+b_1)+\alpha((a_0+b_0)-(a_1+b_1)), a_0+b_0]$
$MM_{7,-}$	$[(a_1-b_2)+\alpha((a_0+b_2)-(a_1+b_0)),\ a_0-b_0]$
$MM_{8,+}$	$[(a_1+b_0)+\alpha(a_0-a_1), a_0+b_0]$
$MM_{8,-}$	$[(a_1-b_0)+\alpha(a_0-a_1), a_0-b_0]$
$MM_{10,-}$	$[a_0-b_0,(a_2-b_1)-\alpha((a_2+b_0)-(a_0+b_1))]$
$MM_{11,+}$	$[a_0+b_0,(a_2+b_2)-\alpha((a_2+b_2)-(a_0+b_0))]$
$MM_{12,+}$	$[a_0+b_0,(a_2+b_0)-\alpha(a_2-a_0)]$
$MM_{12,-}$	$[a_0-b_0,(a_2-b_0)-\alpha(a_2-a_0)]$
$MM_{14,+}$	$[(a_0+b_1)+\alpha(b_0-b_1), a_0+b_0]$
$MM_{14,-}$	$[a_0-b_0,(a_0-b_1)-\alpha(b_0-b_1)]$
$MM_{15,+}$	$[a_0+b_0,(a_0+b_2)-\alpha(b_2-b_0)]$
$MM_{15,-}$	$[(a_0-b_2)+\alpha(b_2-b_0), a_0-b_0]$
$MM_{16,+}$	$[a_0+b_0, a_0+b_0]$
$MM_{16,-}$	$[a_0-b_0, a_0-b_0]$

"addition" and 8 models for "subtraction"). The same situation with the reduction of the direct models' number illustrated by Table 3, where reduced library is represented by 16 direct models $\mu_{\underset{\sim}{C}}(x)$ for the resulting fuzzy sets $\underset{\sim}{C} = \underset{\sim}{A}(\pm)\underset{\sim}{B}$ (8 models for "addition" and 8 models for "subtraction"). Let us consider an example for realisation of the arithmetic operation "addition" and "subtraction" for pair $(\underset{\sim}{A},\underset{\sim}{B})$ with the following left-asymmetrical $\underset{\sim}{A}$ and right-asymmetrical $\underset{\sim}{B}$ TrFNs:

$$\underset{\sim}{A}=(5,5,12)\,,\ \underset{\sim}{B}=(6,14,14)$$

and the corresponding masks

$$\text{Mask}\ \underset{\sim}{A}=\{s,n\}=\{1,0\}\,,\ \text{Mask}\ \underset{\sim}{B}=\{m,r\}=\{0,1\}\,.$$

For this combination of the TrFNs only the condition (16) is existing. Using the proposed algorithm (Figure 1) we can determine in an automatic mode the mask of the pair $(\underset{\sim}{A},\underset{\sim}{B})$

$$\text{Mask}\ (\underset{\sim}{A},\underset{\sim}{B})=\{s,n,m,r\}=\{1,0,0,1\}$$

and the corresponding models $MM_{1,+}$ (for the arithmetic operation "addition") and $MM_{10,-}$ (for the arithmetic operation "subtraction") from the reduced (8+8)-component Library of the models (Table2, Table 3), which includes preliminary synthesized inverse $C_\alpha=[c_1(\alpha),c_2(\alpha)]$ and direct $\mu_{\underset{\sim}{C}}(x)$ models. If we use (16+16)-component Library [19], then we can get the corresponding mathematical model MM_{10} for both operations, but, for example, for the arithmetic operation "addition" we will obtain the same results: the MF $\mu_{\underset{\sim}{C}}(x)$ of the resulting TrFN $\underset{\sim}{C}=\underset{\sim}{A}(+)\underset{\sim}{B}$ and inverse model $C_\alpha=[c_1(\alpha),c_2(\alpha)]$ that can be presented for both $MM_{1,+}$ (from the (8+8)-component Library) and $MM_{10,+}$ (from the (16+16)-component Library [19]) in the same style as follows

$$\mu_{\underset{\sim}{C}}(x)=\mu_{\underset{\sim}{A}(+)\underset{\sim}{B}}(x)=\begin{cases}0, & \forall(x\le 11)\cup(x\ge 26)\\ (x-11)/8, & \forall(11<x\le 19)\\ (26-x)/7, & \forall(19<x<26)\end{cases}.$$

$$C_\alpha=A_\alpha(+)B_\alpha=[11+8\alpha,26-7\alpha]\,.$$

Table 3. Reduced Library of the direct models $\mu_{\underset{\sim}{C}}(x)$ for resulting TFN $\underset{\sim}{C} = \underset{\sim}{A}(\pm)\underset{\sim}{B}$

$MM_{i,+,-}$	$\mu_{\underset{\sim}{C}}(x)$
$MM_{1,+}$	$0, \quad \forall(x \le a_1 + b_1) \cup (x \ge a_2 + b_2)$ $(x - a_1 - b_1)/(a_0 + b_0 - a_1 - b_1), \forall(a_1 + b_1 < x \le a_0 + b_0)$ $(a_2 + b_2 - x)/(a_2 + b_2 - a_0 - b_0), \forall(a_0 + b_0 < x < a_2 + b_2)$
$MM_{1,-}$	$0, \quad \forall(x \le a_1 - b_2) \cup (x \ge a_2 - b_1)$ $(x - a_1 + b_2)/(a_0 + b_2 - a_1 - b_0), \forall(a_1 - b_2 < x \le a_0 - b_0)$ $(a_2 - b_1 - x)/(a_2 + b_0 - a_0 - b_1), \forall(a_0 - b_0 < x < a_2 - b_1)$
$MM_{6,+}$	$0, \quad \forall(x \le a_1 + b_1) \cup (x > a_0 + b_0)$ $(x - a_1 - b_1)/(a_0 + b_0 - a_1 - b_1), \forall(a_1 + b_1 < x < a_0 + b_0)$ $1, \quad \forall(x = a_0 + b_0)$
$MM_{7,-}$	$0, \quad \forall(x \le a_1 - b_2) \cup (x \ge a_0 - b_0)$ $(x - a_1 + b_2)/(a_0 + b_2 - a_1 - b_0), \forall(a_1 - b_2 < x < a_0 - b_0)$ $1, \quad \forall(x = a_0 - b_0)$
$MM_{8,+}$	$0, \quad \forall(x \le a_1 + b_0) \cup (x > a_0 + b_0)$ $(x - a_1 - b_0)/(a_0 - a_1), \quad \forall(a_1 + b_0 < x < a_0 + b_0)$ $1, \quad \forall(x = a_0 + b_0)$
$MM_{8,-}$	$0, \quad \forall(x \le a_1 - b_0) \cup (x \ge a_0 - b_0)$ $(x - a_1 + b_0)/(a_0 - a_1), \forall(a_1 - b_0 < x < a_0 - b_0)$ $1, \quad \forall(x = a_0 - b_0)$
$MM_{10,-}$	$0, \quad \forall(x < a_0 - b_0) \cup (x \ge a_2 - b_1)$ $1, \quad \forall(x = a_0 - b_0)$ $(a_2 - b_1 - x)/(a_2 + b_0 - a_0 - b_1), \forall(a_0 - b_0 < x < a_2 - b_1)$
$MM_{11,+}$	$0, \quad \forall(x < a_0 + b_0) \cup (x \ge a_2 + b_2)$ $1, \quad \forall(x = a_0 + b_0)$ $(a_2 + b_2 - x)/(a_2 + b_2 - a_0 - b_0), \forall(a_0 + b_0 < x < a_2 + b_0)$

Table 3. (Continued)

$MM_{12,+}$	$0, \quad \forall(x < a_0 + b_0) \cup (x \geq a_2 + b_0)$ $1, \quad \forall(x = a_0 + b_0)$ $(a_2 + b_0 - x)/(a_2 - a_0), \forall(a_0 + b_0 < x < a_2 + b_0)$
$MM_{12,-}$	$0, \quad \forall(x < a_0 - b_0) \cup (x \geq a_2 - b_0)$ $1, \quad \forall(x = a_0 - b_0)$ $(a_2 - b_0 - x)/(a_2 - a_0), \forall(a_0 - b_0 < x < a_2 - b_0)$
$MM_{14,+}$	$0, \quad \forall(x < a_0 + b_1) \cup (x > a_0 + b_0)$ $(x - a_0 - b_1)/(b_0 - b_1), \forall(a_0 + b_1 \leq x < a_0 + b_0)$ $1, \quad \forall(x = a_0 + b_0)$
$MM_{14,-}$	$0, \quad \forall(x < a_0 - b_0) \cup (x \geq a_0 - b_1)$ $1, \quad \forall(x = a_0 - b_0)$ $(a_0 - b_1 - x)/(b_0 - b_1), \quad \forall(a_0 - b_0 < x < a_0 - b_1)$
$MM_{15,+}$	$0, \quad \forall(x < a_0 + b_0) \cup (x > a_0 + b_2)$ $1, \quad \forall(x = a_0 + b_0)$ $(a_0 + b_2 - x)/(b_2 - b_0), \quad \forall(a_0 + b_0 < x < a_0 + b_2)$
$MM_{15,-}$	$0, \quad \forall(x \leq a_0 - b_2) \cup (x > a_0 - b_0)$ $(x - a_0 + b_2)/(b_2 - b_0), \forall(a_1 - b_2 < x < a_0 - b_0)$ $1, \quad \forall(x = a_0 - b_0)$
$MM_{16,+}$	$0, \quad \forall(x < a_0 + b_0) \cup (x > a_0 + b_0)$ $1, \quad \forall(x = a_0 + b_0)$
$MM_{16,-}$	$0, \forall(x < a_0 - b_0) \cup (x > a_0 - b_0)$ $1, \forall(x = a_0 - b_0)$

In the case of the arithmetic operation "subtraction" for these TrFNs $\underset{\sim}{A} = (5, 5, 12)$ and $\underset{\sim}{B} = (6, 14, 14)$ we can get the direct and inverse resulting models, using models $MM_{10,-}$ of the Library (Table 2, Table 3), in the following style:

$$\mu_{\underset{\sim}{C}}(x)=\mu_{\underset{\sim}{A}(-)\underset{\sim}{B}}(x)=\begin{cases}0, & \forall(x<-9)\cup(x\geq 6)\\ 1, & \forall(x=-9)\\ (6-x)/15, & \forall(-9<x<6)\end{cases}.$$

$$C_\alpha=A_\alpha(-)B_\alpha=[-9,\ 6-15\alpha].$$

For the desired arguments, for example, $x_1^*=21$ and $x_2^*=4$, we can calculate the corresponding values according to (18) and (20):

a. for the arithmetic operation "addition"
$\mu_{\underset{\sim}{C}}(x_1^*)=\mu_{\underset{\sim}{A}(+)\underset{\sim}{B}}(21)=5/7=0.7143;\quad \mu_{\underset{\sim}{C}}(x_2^*)=\mu_{\underset{\sim}{A}(+)\underset{\sim}{B}}(4)=0;$

b. for the arithmetic operation "subtraction"
$\mu_{\underset{\sim}{C}}(x_1^*)=\mu_{\underset{\sim}{A}(-)\underset{\sim}{B}}(21)=0;\quad \mu_{\underset{\sim}{C}}(x_2^*)=\mu_{\underset{\sim}{A}(-)\underset{\sim}{B}}(4)=2/15=0.1333.$

Another example with the "addition" and "subtraction" of the left-asymmetrical $\underset{\sim}{A}=(5,5,12)$ and left-asymmetrical $\underset{\sim}{B}=(6,6,14)$ TrFNs shows that only condition (14) is fulfilment. In this case Mask $(\underset{\sim}{A},\underset{\sim}{B})=\{s,n,m,r\}=\{1,0,1,0\}$ and the mathematical models $MM_{11,+}$ and $MM_{1,-}$ (from the (8+8)-component Library) will be chosen by corresponding algorithm, presented as Figure 1 or abovementioned Perl-code. The direct $\mu_{\underset{\sim}{C}}(x)$ and inverse $C_\alpha=[c_1(\alpha),c_2(\alpha)]$ models of the resulting TrFNs $\underset{\sim}{A}(+)\underset{\sim}{B}$ and $\underset{\sim}{A}(-)\underset{\sim}{B}$ can be presented (Table 2, Table 3) as follows:

$$\mu_{\underset{\sim}{C}}(x)=\mu_{\underset{\sim}{A}(+)\underset{\sim}{B}}(x)=\begin{cases}0, & \forall(x<11)\cup(x\geq 26)\\ 1, & \forall(x=11)\\ (26-x)/15, & \forall(11<x<26)\end{cases}.$$

$$C_\alpha=A_\alpha(+)B_\alpha=[11,\ 26-15\alpha],$$

$$\mu_{\underset{\sim}{C}}(x)=\mu_{\underset{\sim}{A}(-)\underset{\sim}{B}}(x)=\begin{cases}0, & \forall(x<-9)\cup(x\geq 6)\\ (x+9)/8, & \forall(-9\leq x<-1)\\ (6-x)/7, & \forall(-1\leq x<6)\end{cases}.$$

$$C_\alpha = A_\alpha(-)B_\alpha = [-9+8\alpha,\ 6-7\alpha].$$

Modeling results for the different pairs of the TrFNs (Table 1) confirm the high efficiency of the proposed algorithm (Figure 1) and reduced Library with corresponding size: (8+8)-models.

6. Applied Directions for Implementation of the Reduced Library of Fuzzy Analytic Models

Addition and subtraction of the fuzzy sets are important operations in the fuzzy arithmetic [9, 10, 13, 19]. The implementation of the developed direct analytic models (17)-(32) for calculation of the resulting MFs $\mu_{\underset{\sim}{C}}(x)$ according to the asymmetrical TrFNs with various shape of MF, presented in Table 1, allows using one step automation mode for operations $\underset{\sim}{C} = \underset{\sim}{A}(+)\underset{\sim}{B}$ or $\underset{\sim}{C} = \underset{\sim}{A}(-)\underset{\sim}{B}$. In many practical and theoretical cases, such direct analytic models $\mu_{\underset{\sim}{C}}(x) = \mu_{\underset{\sim}{A}(+)\underset{\sim}{B}}(x)$ and $\mu_{\underset{\sim}{C}}(x) = \mu_{\underset{\sim}{A}(-)\underset{\sim}{B}}(x)$ may have efficient introducing to the evaluation and decision support processes. In [15] authors have considered several examples of the real-life problems, especially for the decision-making in solving capacitive vehicle routing problem with fuzzy demands (CVRPFD), ship transportation, problems in the agricultural sector and so on [1, 14, 26, 39, 41, 42].

In general problem statement for CVRPFD [38, 40], the coordinates of the nodes and vehicles' capacity $D_{\max}$ may be known, but the demands in the corresponding nodes may be uncertain. One of the most important vehicle routing problems [39] is a routing problem for bunkering tankers [14, 40, 41], which should provide bunkering (transportation and unloading) operations for various served (ordered) ships, located in the different marine ports and open sea points. Marine practice shows that very often the information about fuel demands of served ships and ports is uncertain. Typically the ship's owner sends the order for quantity of fuel supply to bunkering company as an approximate value. It is possible to represent such kind of orders as fuzzy demands, for example, as fuzzy numbers with triangular membership function [14, 40, 41]. The efficiency of the preliminary bunkering operations planning can be evaluated by the possibility to serve all ships' orders with maximal value of the unloaded fuel quantity and with the minimal length of the total tankers' routes.

The VRP with fuzzy demands $\underset{\sim}{q}_j = \left(\underline{q}_j, \hat{q}_j, \overline{q}_j\right)$ in nodes is considered in [14, 38, 40, 41], where $\hat{q}_j$ is a value of membership function of triangular fuzzy number $\tilde{q}_j$ with $\mu\left(\hat{q}_j\right)=1$; $\underline{q}_j$ and $\overline{q}_j$ are the lowest and highest possible values of the corresponding demand, respectively, $\mu\left(\underline{q}_j\right)=0$, $\mu\left(\overline{q}_j\right)=0$. In many cases, uncertain demands can be presented by symmetrical/asymmetrical triangular fuzzy numbers, for example:

j-th uncertain demand "*the value of uploading fuel will be not less than value G*" can be represented by left-asymmetrical triangular fuzzy number $\underset{\sim}{q}_j$:

$$\underset{\sim}{q}_j = \left(\underline{q}_j, \hat{q}_j, \overline{q}_j\right) = \left(\hat{q}_j, \hat{q}_j, \overline{q}_j\right),$$

$$Mask\left(\underset{\sim}{q}_j\right) = \{s,n\} = \{1,0\},$$

where $\hat{q}_j = G$; $\overline{q}_j > G$;

($j+1$)-th uncertain demand "*the value of uploading fuel will be not greater than S*" can be represented by right-asymmetrical triangular fuzzy number $\underset{\sim}{q}_{j+1}$:

$$\underset{\sim}{q}_{j+1} = \left(\underline{q}_{j+1}, \hat{q}_{j+1}, \overline{q}_{j+1}\right) = \left(\underline{q}_{j+1}, \hat{q}_{j+1}, \hat{q}_{j+1}\right),$$

$$Mask\left(\underset{\sim}{q}_{j+1}\right) = \{s,n\} = \{0,1\},$$

where $\hat{q}_{j+1} = S$; $\underline{q}_{j+1} < S$;

($j+2$)-th uncertain demand "*the value of uploading fuel will be approximately between the values P_1 and P_2*" can be represented by symmetrical triangular fuzzy number $\underset{\sim}{q}_{j+2}$:

$$\underset{\sim}{q}_{j+2} = \left(\underline{q}_{j+2}, \hat{q}_{j+2}, \overline{q}_{j+2}\right),$$

$$Mask\left(\underset{\sim}{q}_{j+2}\right)=\{s,n\}=\{0,0\},$$

where $\underline{q}_{j+2}=P_1$; $\overline{q}_{j+2}=P_2$; $P_1<\hat{q}_{j+2}<P_2$;

(j+3)-th uncertain demand "*the value of uploading fuel will be U*" can be represented by asymmetrical triangular fuzzy number $\underset{\sim}{q}_{j+3}$:

$$\underset{\sim}{q}_{j+3}=\left(\underline{q}_{j+3},\hat{q}_{j+3},\overline{q}_{j+3}\right)=\left(\hat{q}_{j+3},\hat{q}_{j+3},\hat{q}_{j+3}\right),$$

$$Mask\left(\underset{\sim}{q}_{j+3}\right)=\{s,n\}=\{1,1\},$$

where $\hat{q}_{j+3}=\underline{q}_{j+3}=\overline{q}_{j+3}=U$.

Solving such kind of decision-making problems deals with the implementation of (a) the arithmetic operation "addition" for calculating summarized quantity of cargo $\sum_{j=1}^{r}\underset{\sim}{q}_j$ in serial (r) ports with fuzzy demands $\underset{\sim}{q}_1,\underset{\sim}{q}_2,...,\underset{\sim}{q}_r$:

$$\sum_{j=1}^{r}\underset{\sim}{q}_j=\underset{\sim}{q}_1(+)\underset{\sim}{q}_2(+)...(+)\underset{\sim}{q}_j(+)\underset{\sim}{q}_{j+1}(+)...(+)\underset{\sim}{q}_r$$

and (b) the corresponding arithmetic operation "subtraction" for calculating the remaining cargo $\Delta\underset{\sim}{D}$ at tanker-refueler after serving several points of destinations with the fuzzy demands [14, 19, 40]:

$$\Delta\underset{\sim}{D}=D_{\max}-\sum_{j=1}^{r}\underset{\sim}{q}_j\ .$$

All these demands $\underset{\sim}{q}_1,\underset{\sim}{q}_2,...,\underset{\sim}{q}_r$ may have various shapes of the MFs for their representation as triangular fuzzy models. The usage of the developed in Section 5 fuzzy models and algorithm allows increasing the efficiency of the decision-making processes for planning and optimization of tanker's routes [14, 40, 41].

In some cases for efficiency evaluation of the preliminary planned routes with fuzzy demands at nodes (after solving CVRPFD) researchers use the simulation procedure [14, 38], based on (a) the multi-times random generation of the crisp values of the demands at nodes, (b) the calculation of the statistical data of the successful (a tanker can visit all preliminary planned nodes on the corresponding route) and unsuccessful (a tanker not being able to visit all the preliminary planned nodes on the corresponding route and should return to the depot for uploading additional fuel and to visit again unserved nodes), and (c) the evaluation of the total length of the preliminary planned and additional returned routes. The example of the fuzzy demand $\underset{\sim}{q}_j$ and real crisp demand B_j at node A (Figure 2) illustrates that the real demand B_j belongs to the triangular fuzzy set $\underset{\sim}{q}_j = \underset{\sim}{A}$ with the grade of the membership function $\mu_{\underset{\sim}{A}}\left(B_j\right) \approx 0.435$. In every investigation case for the evaluation of any preliminary planning route it is necessary to use the direct model (Table 3) of the remaining fuel quantity at the bunkering tanker (as fuzzy number $\Delta \underset{\sim}{D}$) and calculate the grade of its membership for modeling the random value of the crisp demand. For example, in [38] authors used 500 random models of the fuzzy and real demands for evaluation of the efficiency of the preliminary planned routes and in [14] authors used 10^4 fuzzy and real demands' simulation models. The index of efficiency in both cases [14, 38] deals with the total length of the preliminary planned and additional returned routes for realization of all bunkering operations on the corresponding routes.

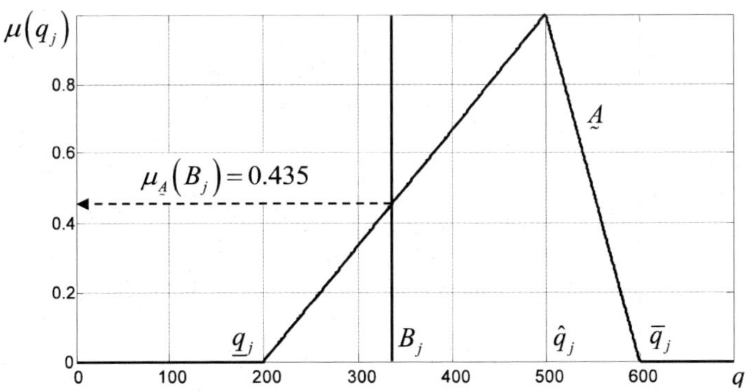

Figure 2. Simulation models of the fuzzy demand $\underset{\sim}{q}_j$ and corresponding real demand B_j at the node A.

The resulting fuzzy models and algorithm outlined in this chapter may be successfully implemented for the arithmetic operations with fuzzy input data that can be presented as TrFNs with various shapes of MFs. Among the potential applications of such kind of fuzzy information processing [19] is a design of the decision support systems for solving problems of knowledge testing, reconfigurable computerized units creating, fire modeling, ship scheduling, berth allocation, minimal risk transport logistics [4, 23, 27, 28, 30, 34] as well as routing and scheduling in a liquefied natural gas shipping problem with the inventory and berth constraints. It is also highly applicable for the decision making in business process management for companies with distributed structures, estimation of software development costs, medical diagnostics, practical project planning, control and management, investment decision process in uncertainty, political decision making, sport and cultural management, financial analysis, problem of uncertainty in socio-economic systems [3, 12, 24, 28, 31, 32] and others.

CONCLUSION

The usage of the developed analytical models of asymmetrical TrFNs (Table 2, Table 3) allows improving a row of very important computational characteristics, in particular, the accuracy of calculations, time of modeling and program implementation of the formed models in the comparison with the step-by-step arithmetic operations based on the algorithms of sorting and max-min convolutions [13, 19, 33].

Special conditions (14)-(17) are proposed with the purpose of reducing the Library of direct and inverse models as resulting fuzzy sets for arithmetic operations of "addition" and "subtraction" with the asymmetrical TrFNs.

Modeling results for addition and subtraction of different TrFNs with various shapes of MFs confirm the efficiency of the twice-reduced Library of the (8+8) resulting analytic models for different applications.

Reduced Library of the resulting inverse and direct analytic models (Table 2, Table 3) may be successfully implemented for solving a wide set of real-life fuzzy optimization problems, in particular, [2, 3, 12, 24, 28, 31, 32, 37, 45] in medicine, economics, management, social and political sciences, transport logistics, investment, etc.

ACKNOWLEDGMENTS

Authors cordially thank the Fulbright Program (Fulbright Scholar Program and Fulbright Graduate Student Exchange Program), administrated by the Bureau of Educational and Cultural Affairs of the United States Department of State with the cooperation of the Council for International Exchange of Scholars, for the support of their research and study in the USA as well as their US host institutions - Cleveland State University and South Carolina State University.

REFERENCES

[1] Anselin-Avila, E., Gil-Lafuente, A.M.: Fuzzy logic in the strategic analysis: impact of the external factors over business. *International Journal of Business Innovation and Research* 3, no. 5, 515-534 (2009).

[2] Atamanyuk, I.P., Kondratenko, V.Y., Kozlov, O.V., Kondratenko Y.P.: Extrapolation Algorithm of Economic Indicators on the Basis on Nonlinear Canonical Decomposition of Casual Process. *Journal of Computational Optimization in Economics and Finance* 6, Issue 3, Nova Science Publishers, New York, 207-218 (2014).

[3] Atamanyuk, I., Kondratenko, Y.: Calculation Method for a Computer's Diagnostics of Cardiovascular Diseases Based on Canonical Decompositions of Random Sequences. In: ICT in Education, Research and Industrial Applications: Integration, Harmonization and Knowledge Transfer. *Proceedings of the 11th International Conference ICTERI-2015*, S. Batsakis, et al. (Eds), CEUR-WS, Vol. 1356, Lviv, Ukraine, May 14-16, 108-120 (2015).

[4] Drozd, J., Drozd, A.: Models, Methods and Means as Resources for Solving Challenges in Co-Design and Testing of Computer Systems and their Components. *Proceedings of 9th International Conference on Digital Technologies 2013*. Zhilina, Slovak Republic, 29 – 31 May, 225 – 230 (2013).

[5] Gerdt, V.P., Prokopenya, A.N.: Simulation of quantum error correction with Mathematica. Computer Algebra in Scientific Computing/ CASC'2013, V. P. Gerdt, W. Koepf, E. W. Mayr, E. V. Vorozhtsov (Eds), *Lecture Notes in Computer Science*, vol. 8136, Springer-Verlag, Berlin, pp. 116 – 129 (2013).

[6] Encheva, S., Kondratenko, Y., Solesvik, M.Z., Tumin, S.: Decision Support Systems in Logistics. International Electronic Conference on Computer Science (IeCCS'2007), Nov. 30-Dec. 10, 2007. Book Series: *AIP Conference Proceedings*, Simos, T.E., Psihoyios, G. (Eds), Publisher: American Institute of Physics, USA, pp. 254-256 (2008).

[7] Gao, S., Zhang, Z.: Multiplication Operation on Fuzzy Numbers. Journal of Software 4(4), http://ojs.academypublisher.com/index.php/jsw/article/download/0404331338/1061 (2009).

[8] Gil-Aluja, J., Gil-Lafuente, A.M., Klimova, A.: The Optimization of the Economic Segmentation by Means of Fuzzy Algorithms. *Journal of Computational Optimization in Economics and Finance* 1(3), 169-186 (2011).

[9] Gil-Aluja, J.: *Investment in Uncertainty*. Kluwer Academic Publishers, Dordrecht, Boston, London (1999).

[10] Gil-Lafuente, A.M.: Fuzzy *Logic in Financial Analysis*. Studies in Fuzziness and Soft Computing 175, Springer, Berlin (2005).

[11] Hampel, R., Wagenknecht, M., Chaker N. (Eds.): *Fuzzy Control: Theory and Practice*. Physika-Verlag, Heidelberg, New York (2000).

[12] Jamshidi, M., Kreinovitch, V., Kacprzyk, J. (Eds): *Advance Trends in Soft Computing*. Springer-Verlag, Germany (2013).

[13] Kaufmann, A., Gupta, M.: *Introduction to Fuzzy Arithmetic: Theory and Applications*. Van Nostrand Reinhold Company, New York (1985).

[14] Kondratenko, G.V., Kondratenko, Y.P., Romanov, D.O.: Fuzzy Models for Capacitive Vehicle Routing Problem in Uncertainty. *Proc. 17th International DAAAM Symposium "Intelligent Manufacturing and Automation: Focus on Mechatronics and Robotics,"* pp. 205-206. Vienna, Austria (2006).

[15] Kondratenko, V.: Synthesis of Analytic Models for Computing Operations with Fuzzy Numbers: Operation of Multiplication. *J. Technical News* 1(20), 2(21), 85-90 (2005) (in Ukrainian).

[16] Kondratenko, V.: Increasing Dependability Method for Calculating Operations of Fuzzy Arithmetic. *Radio-Electronic and Computer Systems*, No. 7, 36-40 (2007).

[17] Kondratenko, V., Iablonska, K., Kondratenko, Y.: The Universal Analytical Models of Fuzzy Arithmetic Computing Operations: Direct and Inverse Approach. *17th Zittau East-West Fuzzy Collquium*, Wissenschaftliche Berichte, Heft 106/2010, Nr.2454-2490, pp.112-119 (2010).

[18] Kondratenko, V.Y.: Analysis of Characteristics and Mathematical Model of Result Membership Function for Multiplication of Fuzzy Numbers. *Visnyk of Kherson National Technical University* 1(24), 488-494 (2006) (in Ukrainian).

[19] Kondratenko, Y.P., Kondratenko, N.Y.: Soft Computing Analytic Models for Increasing Efficiency of Fuzzy Information Processing in Decision Support Systems. *Chapter in book: Decision Making: Processes, Behavioral Influences and Role in Business Management*, R. Hudson (Ed.), Nova Science Publishers, New York, 41-78 (2015).

[20] Kondratenko, Y., Kondratenko, V.: Soft Computing Algorithm for Arithmetic Multiplication of Fuzzy Sets Based on Universal Analytic Models. In book: Information and Communication Technologies in Education, Research, and Industrial Application. Series: *Communications in Computer and Information Science* 469, Ermolayev, V. et al. (Eds): ICTERI'2014, Springer International Publishing Switzerland, pp. 49–77 (2014).

[21] Kondratenko, Y.P., Kondratenko, V.Y., Kondratenko, N.Y.: The Method of Analytic Models Synthesis for Resulting Fuzzy Sets in Realization of Fuzzy Arithmetic Operations. Ukraine *Patent for Utility Model №68118*, Bulletin №5 (2012).

[22] Kondratenko, Y.P., Sidenko, Ie.V.: Decision-Making Based on Fuzzy Estimation of Quality Level for Cargo Delivery. In book: Recent Developments and New Directions in Soft Computing. *Studies in Fuzziness and Soft Computing* 317, Zadeh, L.A. et al. (Eds), Springer International Publishing Switzerland, pp. 331-344, (2014).

[23] Kondratenko, Y.P., Sidenko Ie.V.: Design and Reconfiguration of Intelligent Knowledge-Based System for Fuzzy Multi-Criterion Decision Making in Transport Logisticts. *Journal of Computational Optimization in Economics and Finance* 6, Issue 3, Nova Science Publishers, New York, 229-242 (2014).

[24] Kotov, Y.B.: *New Mathematical Approaches to the Problems of Medical Diagnostics*. Editorial EPCC, Moscow (2004) (in Russian).

[25] Lodwick, W.A., Kacprzhyk, J. (Eds): Fuzzy Optimization. Studies in Fuzziness and Soft Computing 254, Springer-Verlag, Berlin, Heidelberg (2010).

[26] Lutter, P., Werners, B.: Order acceptance for motorail transportation with uncertain parameters. OR Spectrum 37, no. 2, 431-456 (2015).

[27] Mandel, J., Amram, S., Beezley, J.D., Kelman, G., Kochanski, A.K., Kondratenko, V.Y., Lynn, B.H., Regev, B., Vejmelka, M.: Recent

advances and applications of WRF–SFIRE. *Natural Hazards and Earth System Science* 14, no. 10, 2829-2845 (2014).

[28] Merigo, J.M., Gil-Lafuente, A.M., Yager, R.R.: An overview of fuzzy research with bibliometric indicators. *Applied Soft Computing*, No. 27, 420-433 (2015).

[29] Piegat, A.: *Fuzzy Modeling and Control*. Springer, Heidelberg (2001)

[30] Palagin, A., Opanasenko, V.: Reconfigurable computing technology. *J. Cybernetics and Systems Analysis* 43, no.5, Springer, New York, 675–686 (2007).

[31] Ragin, C.C.: *Fuzzy-Set Social Science*. The University of Chicago Press, Chicago, London (2000).

[32] Ragin, C.C.: *Redesigning Social Inquiry: Fuzzy Sets and Beyond*. The University of Chicago Press, Chicago, London (2008).

[33] Rotshtein, A.P.: *Intellectual Technologies of Identification: Fuzzy Logic, Genetic Algorithms, Neuron Networks*. UNIVERSUM, Vinnitsa (1999) (in Russian).

[34] Shahbazova, S.N.: Application of Fuzzy Sets for Control of Student Knowledge, *An International Journal Applied and Computational Mathematics* 10, no. 1, 195-208 (2011).

[35] Simon, D.: Training fuzzy systems with the extended Kalman filter. *Fuzzy Sets and Systems* 132, 189-199 (2002).

[36] Simon, D.: Sum normal optimization of fuzzy membership functions. *Intern. Journal of Uncertainty, Fuziness and Knowledge-Based Systems* 10, 363-384 (2002).

[37] Tamir, D.E., Rishe, N.D., Kandel A. (Eds): *Fifty Years of Fuzzy Logic and its Applications*. Studies in Fuzziness and Soft Computing 326, Cham-Heidelberg-New Yorl-Dordrecht-London, Springer International Publishing Switzerland (2015).

[38] Teodorovic, D., Pavkovich, G.: The fuzzy set theory approach to the vehicle routing problem when demand at nodes is uncertain. *Fuzzy Sets and Systems* 82, 307-317 (1996).

[39] Toth, P., Vigo, D. (Eds): *The vehicle routing problem*. SIAM, Philadelphia (2002).

[40] Werners, B., Kondratenko, Y.P.: Tanker Routing Problem with Fuzzy Demands of Served Ships. *Int. J. System Research and Information Technologies* 1, 47-64 (2009).

[41] Werners, B., Kondratenko, Y.P.: Fuzzy Multi-Criteria Optimisation for Vehicle Routing with Capacity Constraints and Uncertain Demands. *Proceedings of the International Congress on Cost Control* (17-18

March, 2011, Barcelona, Spain), Publ. by ACCID/ASEPUC, Barcelona, pp. 145-159 (2011).
[42] Werners, B., Drawe, M. (2003): Capacitated vehicle routing problem with fuzzy demand. In book: *Fuzzy sets based heuristics for optimization*, Verdegay, J.-L. (Ed), Berlin, 317–335 (2003).
[43] Yampolsky, L.S., Tkach, B.P., Lisovychenko, O.I.: *Artificial Intelligence Systems for Planning, Modeling and Management.* Publ. House "Personal," Kyiv (2011).
[44] Zadeh, L.A.: Fuzzy Sets. Information and Control 8, 338-353 (1965).
[45] Zadeh, L.A., Abbasov, A.M., Yager, R.R., Shahbazova, S.N., Reformat, M.Z. (Eds): *Recent Developments and New Directions in Soft Computing*. Studies in Fuzziness and Soft Computing 317, Springer (2014).

BIOGRAPHICAL SKETCHES

Yuriy P. Kondratenko

Affiliation: Department of Intelligent Information Systems, Petro Mohyla Black Sea State University, Ukraine; Department of Electrical Engineering and Computer Science, Cleveland State University, USA (host university)

Education: Engineer diploma, PhD, Doctor of Science, Professor

Address: Petro Mohyla Black Sea State University, 10, 68th Desantnykiv Str., Mykolaiv, 54003, Ukraine; Cleveland State University, 2121 Euclid Avenue, SH 332, Cleveland, OH, 44115, USA

Research and Professional Experience: 30 years of experience as a researcher in robotics, automation, sensors and control systems, intelligent decision support systems, fuzzy logic, soft computing, elements and devices of computing systems; principal researcher of several international research projects with Spain, P.R. of China, Germany et al.; multi-years' experience in the education field as lecturer, senior lecturer, associate professor, professor, head of department.

Professional Appointments: Professor at the Department of Intelligent Information Systems, Petro Mohyla Black Sea State University, Ukraine;

Fulbright Visiting Scholar at the Department of Electrical Engineering and Computer Science, Cleveland State University, USA (2015/2016).

Honors: Honor Inventor of Ukraine (2008), Corr. Academician of Royal European Academy of Doctors, Barcelona, Spain (2000), member of the international associations GAMM, DAAAM, AMSE UA-PL and PBD - Honor Society of International Scholars, member of the National Committee of Ukraine on Automatic Control; international grants and scholarships for conducting research at Cleveland State University, USA (Fulbright Program – 2015/2016), Nazareth College and Cleveland State University, USA (IREX – 2003), Ruhr-University Bochum, Germany (DAAD - 2000, 2010), Institute of Automation of Chongqing University, P.R.China (1988-1989).

Publications Last 3 Years (only in English):

Kondratenko, Y.P., Duro, R. (Eds): *Advances in Intelligent Robotics and Collaboration Automation.* River Publishers Series on Automation, Control and Robotics, River Publishers, Denmark (2015)

Kondratenko, Y.P., Kondratenko, V.Y.: Advanced Trends in Design of Slip Displacement Sensors for Intelligent Robots. *Chapter in book: Advances in Intelligent Robotics and Collaboration Automation*, Kondratenko, Y.P., Duro, R. (Eds), River Publishers Series on Automation, Control and Robotics, River Publishers, Denmark, 167-191 (2015)

Kondratenko, Y.P.: Model-Oriented Approach and Fuzzy Decision Support Systems for Evaluation of Science-Economic Realities and Perspectives in S2B and B2S. In book: Ciencia y Realidades Económicas: Reto del Mundo Post-Crisis a la Actividad Investigadora. *X Sesión Internacional de la Real Academia de Ciencias Económicas y Financieras, celebrada en Barcelona el 18 de noviembre de 2015.* Barcelona: Real Academia de Ciencias Economicas y Financieras, 89-112 (2015)

Kondratenko, Y.P., Kondratenko, N.Y.: Soft Computing Analytic Models for Increasing Efficiency of Fuzzy Information Processing in Decision Support Systems. *Chapter in book: Decision Making: Processes, Behavioral Influences and Role in Business Management*, Hudson, R. (Ed), NOVA Science Publishers, New York, 41-78 (2015)

Kondratenko, Y.P., Kondratenko, V.Y., Klymenko, L.P., Kondratenko, G.V., Shvets, E.A.: Sensing of Intelligent Robots Based on Applications of Tactile Slip Displacement Sensors. *Sensors and Transducers* 187, Issue 4, 29-38 (2015)

Kondratenko, Y., Korobko, O., Kozlov, O., Gerasin, O., Topalov, A.: PLC Based System for Remote Liquids Level Control with Radar Sensor. *Proceedings of the 2015 IEEE 8th International Conference on Intelligent Data Acquisition and Advanced Computing Systems: Technology and Applications (IDAACS),* Warsaw, Poland, September 24–26, Volume 1, 47-52 (2015)

Kondratenko, Y. P.: Robotics, Automation and Information Systems: Future Perspectives and Correlation with Culture, Sport and Life Science. In book: Decision Making and Knowledge Decision Support Systems. *Lecture Notes in Economics and Mathematical Systems* 675, Gil-Lafuente, A.M., Zopounidis, C. (Eds), Springer International Publishing Switzerland, 43–56 (2015)

Atamanyuk, I.P., Kondratenko, Y.P.: Method of Modeling, Identification and Prediction of Random Sequences Based on the Nonlinear Canonical Decomposition. *Tribuna Plural: La revista cientifica.* Num. 6, 2/2015, Reial Academia de Doctors, Barcelona,: 77 – 114 (2015)

Kondratenko, Y., Korobko, V., Korobko, O., Gerasin, O.: Pulse-Phase Control System for Temperature Stabilization of Thermoacoustic Engine Model Driven by the Waste Heat Energy. *Proceedings of the 2015 IEEE 8th International Conference on Intelligent Data Acquisition and Advanced Computing Systems: Technology and Applications (IDAACS)*, Warsaw, Poland, September 24–26, Volume 1, 58-61 (2015)

Atamanyuk, I., Kondratenko, Y.: Calculation Method for a Computer's Diagnostics of Cardiovascular Diseases Based on Canonical Decompositions of Random Sequences. In book: ICT in Education, Research and Industrial Applications: Integration, Harmonization and Knowledge Transfer. *Proceedings of the 11th International Conference ICTERI-2015*, S.Batsakis, H.C. Mayr, V.Yakovyna, M. Nikitchenko, G. Zholtkevych, V. Kharchenko, H. Kravtsov, V. Kobets, V. Peschanenko, V. Ermolayev, Y. Bobalo, A. Spivakovsky (Eds), CEUR-WS, Vol. 1356, Lviv, Ukraine, May 14-16, 108-120 (2015)

Kondratenko, Y., Topalov, A., Gerasin, O.: Analysis and Modeling of the Slip Signal's Registration Processes Based on Sensors with Multicomponent Sensing Elements. *Proc. of XIIIth International Conference "The Experience of Designing and Application of CAD Systems in Microelectronics,"* CADSM 2015, 19-23 Febr., 2015, Polyana-Svalyava, Ukraine, 109-112 (2015)

Atamanyuk, I., Kondratenko, Y.: Computer's Analysis Method and Reliability Assessment of Fault-Tolerance Operation of Information Systems. In book: ICT in Education, Research and Industrial Applications: Integration, Harmonization and Knowledge Transfer. *Proceedings of the 11th International Conference ICTERI-2015*, S. Batsakis, H.C. Mayr, V. Yakovyna, M. Nikitchenko, G. Zholtkevych, V. Kharchenko, H. Kravtsov, V. Kobets, Vladimir Peschanenko, V. Ermolayev, Y. Bobalo, A.S pivakovsky (Eds.), CEUR-WS, Vol. 1356, Lviv, Ukraine, May 14-16, 507-522 (2015)

Kondratenko, Y.P., Gerasin, O.S., Topalov, A.M.: Modern Sensing Systems of Intelligent Robots Based on Multi-Component Slip Displacement Sensors. *Proceedings of the 2015 IEEE 8th International Conference on Intelligent Data Acquisition and Advanced Computing Systems: Technology and Applications (IDAACS),* Warsaw, Poland, September 24–26, Volume 2, 902–907 (2015)

Atamanyuk, I., Kondratenko, Y., Shebanin, V., Mirgorod, V.: Method of Polynomial Predictive Control of Fail-Safe Operation of Technical Systems. *Proc. XIIIth International Conference "The Experience of Designing and Application of CAD Systems in Microelectronics,"* CADSM 2015, 19-23 Febr., 2015, Polyana-Svalyava, Ukraine, 248-251 (2015)

Kondratenko, Y.P., Sidenko, Ie.V.: Decision-Making Based on Fuzzy Estimation of Quality Level for Cargo Delivery. In book: Recent Developments and New Directions in Soft Computing. *Studies in Fuzziness and Soft Computing* 317, Zadeh, L.A. et al. (Eds), Springer International Publishing Switzerland, 331-344 (2014)

Kondratenko, Y., Kondratenko, V.: Soft Computing Algorithm for Arithmetic Multiplication of Fuzzy Sets Based on Universal Analytic Models. In book: Information and Communication Technologies in Education, Research, and Industrial Application. *Communications in Computer and Information Science* 469, Ermolayev, V. et al. (Eds), ICTERI'2014, Springer International Publishing Switzerland, 49–77 (2014)

Atamanyuk, I., Kondratenko, Y., Shebanin, V.: Method for Determining the Optimal Performance of Polynomial Degree Canonical Expansion for Recognition of Random Sequences, Modern Problems of Radio Engineering, Telecommunications and Computer Science. *Proc. of the XIIth Intern. Conf. TCSET'2014* (February 25 – March 1, 2014, Lviv-Slavske, Ukraine), Lviv: Publ. House of Lviv Polytechnic, 224-225 (2014)

Kondratenko, Y.P.: Revolution in Computer Science and Engineering and Its Impact on Evolution of Higher Education. In book: Revolucion, Evolucion E Involucion En El Futuro De Los Sistemas Sociales. *IX Sesion*

Internacional Celebrada en Barcelona el 11 de Noiembre de 2014, Real Academia de Ciencias Economicas y Financieras, Barcelona, 127-160 (2014)

Kondratenko, Y., Sidenko, Ie.: Methods of Aggregative Processing of Linguistic Information in Decision Making Processes. Modern Problems of Radio Engineering, Telecommunications and Computer Science. *Proc. of the XIIth Intern. Conf. TCSET'2014* (February 25 – March 1, Lviv-Slavske, Ukraine), Lviv: Publ. House of Lviv Polytechnic, 670-671 (2014)

Atamanyuk, I., Kondratenko, Y.: Algorithm of optimum linear extrapolation of vector casual sequence with complete account of cross-correlation connections for every constituent. MOTROL. Commission of Motorization and Energetics in Agriculture. *An International Journal on Operation of Farm and Agri-Food Industry Machinery* 16, No 2, Lublin-Rzeszow, 265-268 (2014)

Kondratenko, Y.P., Kozlov, O.V.: Ecopyrogenesis Automated Technological Complexes for Solving the Energy Problems of the Region's Economy. *J. Computational Optimization in Economics and Finance* 6, Issue 3, Nova Science Publishers, New York, 219-227 (2014)

Kondratenko, Y., Korobko, V., Korobko, O.: Microcontroller System of Temperature Stabilization for Investigation of Thermoacoustic Engine Model Driven by the Waste Heat Energy. Modern Problems of Radio Engineering, Telecommunications and Computer Science. *Proc. of the XIIth Intern. Conf. TCSET'2014* (February 25 – March1, 2014, Lviv-Slavske, Ukraine), Lviv: Publ. House of Lviv Polytechnic, 229-230 (2014)

Atamanyuk, I., Kondratenko, Y., Sirenko, N.: Management of an Agricultural Enterprise on the Basis of Its Economic State Forecasting. *Quantitative Methods in Economics* XV, No. 2, Warsaw, Poland, 7–16 (2014)

Kondratenko, Y., Korobko, O., Kozlov, O., Gerasin, O., Topalov, A.: Measurement of Liquid Level in Tanks under Non-Stationary Conditions Based on Radar Sensor System. Modern Problems of Radio Engineering, Telecommunications and Computer Science. *Proc. of the XIIth Intern. Conf. TCSET'2014* (February 25 – March 1, 2014, Lviv-Slavske, Ukraine), Lviv: Publ. House of Lviv Polytechnic, 797-798 (2014)

Kondratenko, Y.P., Kozlov, O.V., Klymenko, L.P., Kondratenko, G.V.: Synthesis and Research of Neuro-Fuzzy Model of Ecopyrogenesis Multi-circuit Circulatory System. Advance Trends in Soft Computing. M. Jamshidi, V. Kreinovich, J. Kazprzyk (Eds), Springer, Series: *Studies in Fuzziness and Soft Computing* 312, 1-14 (2014)

Atamanyuk, I.P., Kondratenko, V.Y., Kozlov, O.V., Kondratenko, Y.P.: Extrapolation Algorithm of Economic Indicators on the Basis on Nonlinear Canonical Decomposition of Casual Process. *J. Computational Optimization in Economics and Finance* 6, Issue 3, Nova Science Publishers, New York, 207-218 (2014)

Kondratenko, Y.P., Korobko, O.V., Kozlov, O.V.: Synthesis and Optimization of Fuzzy Controller for Thermoacoustic Plant. *Proceedings of the 4th World Conference on Soft Computing*, Berkeley, CA, USA, 147-152 (2014)

Kondratenko, Y.P., Sidenko, Ie.V.: Design and Reconfiguration of Intelligent Knowledge-Based System for Fuzzy Multi-Criterion Decision Making in Transport Logistics. *Journal Computational Optimization in Economics and Finance* 6, Issue 3, Nova Science Publishers, New York, 229-242 (2014)

Kondratenko, Y.P., Kozlov, O.V.: Mathematical Model of Ecopyrogenesis Reactor with Fuzzy Parametrical Identification. *Proceedings of the 4th World Conference on Soft Computing, Berkeley*, CA, USA, pp. 63-68 (2014)

Kondratenko, Y.P., Klymenko, L.P., Sidenko, Ie.V.: Comparative Analysis of Evaluation Algorithms for Decision-Making in Transport Logistics. Advance Trends in Soft Computing. M. Jamshidi, V. Kreinovich, J. Kazprzyk (Eds), Springer, Series: *Studies in Fuzziness and Soft Computing* 312, 203-217 (2014)

Kondratenko, Y.P., Kozlov, O.V., Korobko, O.V.: Development of intelligent controllers for pyrolysis reactor control systems based on their mathematical models. *Transactions of the National University of Shipbuilding*, № 6 (456), Mykolaiv, Ukraine, 66-74 (2014)

Kondratenko, Yu., Korobko, V., Korobko, O., Moskovko, O.: Design of the Fuzzy Control System for the Waste Heat Utilization Plants Driven by the Thermoacoustic Engine. *International Journal of Computing* 13, Issue 2, 88-96 (2014)

Kondratenko, Y., Korobko, V., Korobko, O.: Specialized computer system for control and parametric optimization of thermoacoustic processes. *Chapter in book: Computing in Science and Technology 2013/2014*, M. Kruk (Ed), Monographs in Applied Informatics, Agencia Reklamo-Wydawnicha A. Grzegorczyk, Warsaw, Poland, 2013/2014, 38-54, (2014)

Kondratenko, Y.P., Klymenko, L.P., Al Zu'bi, E.Y.M.: Structural Optimization of Fuzzy Systems' Rules Base and Aggregation Models. *Kybernetes* 42, Iss: 5, 831-843 (2013)

Kondratenko, Y., Klymenko, L., Kondratenko, V., Kondratenko, G., Shvets, E.: Slip Displacement Sensors For Intelligent Robots: Solutions and Models, *Proc. of the 2013 IEEE 7th Int. Conf. on Intelligent Data Acquisition and Advanced Computing Systems (IDAACS),* vol. 2, Sept. 12-14, Berlin, Germany, 861-866 (2013)

Kondratenko, Y.P., Korobko, O.V., Kondratenko, V.Y., Kozlov, O.V.: Optimization Models and Algorithms of Multistage Processes of Liquid Cargoes Transportation for Computer DSS. *Chapter in book: Management Science: Modelle und Methoden zur quantitativen ntscheidungsunterstutzung*, Festschrift zum 60. Geburtstag von Brigitte Werners. K. Armborst, D. Degel, P. Lutter, U. Pietschmann, S. Rachuba, K. Shultz, L. Wiesche (Eds), Verlag Dr. Covac, Hamburg, 241-270 (2013)

Kondratenko, Y., Korobko, V., Korobko, O.: Microprocessor System for Thermoacoustic Plants Efficiency Analysis Based on a Two-Sensor Method. *Sensors and Transducers* 24, Special Issue, August 2013, 35-42 (2013)

Kondratenko, Y.P., Sidenko, Ie.V.: Method of Actual Correction of the Knowledge Database of Fuzzy Decision Support System with Flexible Hierarchical Structure. In book: Computational Techniques in Modeling and Simulation, V. Krasnoproshin, A.M. Gil Lafuente, C. Zopounidis (Eds), Series: *Studies in Financial Optimization and Risk Management*, NOVA Science Publishers, New York, 55-74 (2013)

Kondratenko, Y., Korobko, V., Korobko, O.: Distributed Computer System for Monitoring and Control of Thermoacoustic Processes. *Proc. of the 2013 IEEE 7th Int. Conf. on Intelligent Data Acquisition and Advanced Computing Systems (IDAACS),* vol. 2, Sept. 12-14, 2013, Berlin, Germany, 249-253 (2013)

Atamanyuk, I., Kondratenko, Y.: Information Technology of Determination of Descriptions of Optimum Polynomial Prognosis Algorithm of the State of Technical Systems. MOTROL. Commission of Motorization and Energetics in Agriculture. *An International Journal on Operation of Farm and Agri-Food Industry Machinery* 15, No 2, Lublin-Rzeszow, 47-50 (2013)

Kondratenko, Y.P., Kozlov, O.V., Atamanyuk, I.P., Korobko, O.V.: Computerized Control System for the Pyrolysis Reactor Load Level Based on the Neural Network Controllers. *Chapter in book: Computing in Science and Technology 2012/2013*, T. Kwater, B. Twarog (Eds), Monographs in Applied Informatics, Wydawnictwo Uniwersytety Rzeszowskiego, Rzeszow, Poland, 97-120 (2013)

Nina Y. Kondratenko

Affiliation: International Business, University of South Carolina

Education: MA, MSW, PhD Candidate'18

Address: Department of International Business, Moore School of Business, University of South Carolina, 1014 Greene Street, Columbia, South Carolina, 29208

Research and Professional Experience: international business and corporate social responsibility.

Professional Appointments: PhD student and research assistant at University of South Carolina

Honors: Fulbright Scholarship, FLEX Scholarship, Honor diploma of MA summa cum laude

Publications:

Kondratenko, Y.P., Kondratenko, N.Y.: Soft Computing Analytic Models for Increasing Efficiency of Fuzzy Information Processing in Decision Support Systems. *Chapter in book*: *Decision Making: Processes, Behavioral Influences and Role in Business Management*, Rebecca Hudson (Ed), NOVA Science Publishers, New York, 41-78 (2015)

Kondratenko, Y.P., Kondratenko, V.Y., Kondratenko, N.Y.: Method for formation of analytical models of resulting fuzzy sets in the implementation of fuzzy arithmetic operations. *Ukraine Patent for Utility Model №68118*, Bulletin №5 (2012)

Kondratenko, V.Y., Kondratenko, N.Y., Kondratenko, Y.P.: Computing device for multiplication of fuzzy numbers. *Ukraine Patent for Utility Model №65213*, Bulletin №22 (2011)

Kondratenko, V.Y., Kondratenko, N.Y., Kondratenko, Y.P.: Computing device for division of fuzzy numbers. *Ukraine Patent for Utility Model №65212*, Bulletin №22 (2011)

Kondratenko, Y.P., Kondratenko, N.Y., Kondratenko, V.Y.: Intelligent sensor system. *Ukraine Patent for Utility Model №52080*, Bulletin №15 (2010)

Kondratenko, Y.P., Kondratenko, N.Y., Kondratenko, V.Y.: Method of identification of a compression stress and direction of displacement of an object in the intelligent robot's gripper. *Ukraine Patent for Utility Model №52069*, Bulletin №15 (2010)

Kondratenko, V.Y., Kondratenko, N.Y., Kondratenko, Y.P.: Device for group fuzzy information processing. *Ukraine Patent for Utility Model №48972*, Bulletin №7 (2010)

Kondratenko, V.Y., Kondratenko, N.Y., Kondratenko, Y.P.: Device for group fuzzy information processing. *Ukraine Patent for Utility Model №48962*, Bulletin №7 (2010)

Kondratenko, N.: Latin adjectives picturing positive human traits of feature and their correspondents in French in psychological and linguistic aspects. *Applied linguistics 2010: problems and resolutions, Proceedings of the All-Ukrainian scientific-methodological conference of young researchers*, National University of Shipbuilding, Mykolaiv, Ukraine, 1 page (2010) http://conference.nuos.edu.ua/catalog/lectureDetail; jsessionid=b3345cef0a547ddb62423ac0279c?lectureId=1560&conferenceId=8&isProjectorView=false

Kondratenko, N.: The facilitator's role in the project study process. *Applied linguistics 2009: problems and resolutions, Proceedings of the All-Ukrainian scientific-methodological conference of young researchers*, National University of Shipbuilding, Mykolaiv, Ukraine, pp. 59-62 (2009)

Kondratenko, N.: The importance of the FLEX program for the exchange of world experience. Olbia Forum 2008: Strategies of Ukraine in geopolitical space. *International Scientific-Applied Conference*, Abstracts, vol. 3, 5-8 June, 2008, Yalta, Crimea, Ukraine, p. 70 (2008)

Кондратенко Н.Ю.: Важливість програми обміну майбутніх лідерів для поширення досвіду в міжнародному культуро-освітньому просторі. Міжн. наук.-практ. конф. "Ольвійський форум 2008: Стратегії України в геополітичному просторі," Тези. Част. 3, Ялта, Крим, Україна, 5-8 червня 2008, сс. 71-72 (in Ukrainian).

In: Soft Computing
Editor: Alan Casey
ISBN: 978-1-63485-133-6

Chapter 2

Determination of Stability Number of Layered Slope Using ANFIS, GPR, RVM and ELM

***J. Jagan*[1]*, G. Meghana*[1] *and Pijush Samui*[2,*]**
[1]VIT University, Vellore, India
[3]NIT Patna, Bihar, India

Abstract

While the computational tools have made most charts and graphical approaches antiquated, the proposed soft computing techniques to act as a catalyst medium for determining the stability number (N_s) of layered slope. The objective function of this chapter is to predict the stability number (N_s) of intermediate slope angle by adopting the soft computing techniques like Adaptive Neuro-Fuzzy Inference System (ANFIS), Gaussian Process Regression (GPR), Relevance Vector Machine (RVM) and Extreme Learning Machine (ELM). GPR model depends upon the assumption that the response of the model under consideration is a sample path of an underlying Gaussian random field. Such a stochastic framework is a way to represent the epistemic uncertainty associated with the prediction of the model at an untried set of input parameters. GPR develops a metamodel together with confidence intervals on the predictions. ANFIS adopts fuzzy inference system model to transform the given input to an expected output. Conditional rules, membership

* E-mail: pijushsamui@gmail.com.

functions and logic operators were involved during this transformation. RVM has its strength of its counter-intuitive yet effective way of achieving a sparse representation in data space. ELM has the potential of fast learning with better generalization for accomplishing the optimal and suitable hidden nodes. The utilization of these techniques prevents the hardships and the instabilities of the conventional methods. In addition, the adopted techniques conveyed elegant and encouraging optimal results.

The equations have been constructed for the determining the N_s value in future cases. A comparative study between the developed models has also been employed, in which ELM outperforms the other developed models.

Keywords: slope, Adaptive Neuro-Fuzzy Inference System (ANFIS), Gaussian Process Regression (GPR), Relevance Vector Machine (RVM), Extreme Learning Machine (ELM)

Key Terms and Definitions

Slope: Slope is defined as the angle of inclination of the soil surface from the horizontal. It is very important as it influences the rate at which the runoff flows on the soil surface.

Adaptive Neuro-Fuzzy Inference System (ANFIS): ANFIS constructs a fuzzy inference system (FIS) whose membership function parameters are tuned (adjusted) using either a back propagation algorithm alone or in combination with a least squares type of method. This adjustment allows your fuzzy systems to learn from the data they are modelling.

Gaussian Process Regression (GPR): Gaussian Process is one of the elegant members of stochastic process family. Gaussian process is a non-parametric regression model with an infinite-dimensional generalization of the multivariate normal distribution.

Relevance Vector Machine (RVM): Relevance Vector Machine (RVM) uses Bayesian inference to get the solutions for classification and regression problems. It has same functional form of SVM, but provides the probabilistic classification.

Extreme Learning Machine (ELM): Extreme Learning Machine is the network with single layer of many hidden neurons. The weights connecting to the inputs are designated randomly.

INTRODUCTION

The analysis of slope is the most imperative task when the stability number of slope is being computed. Slope stability is exceedingly vital in the design and construction of highways, open pits, and earthen embankments. The conventional approach to assessing the performance of a slope is to calculate the factor of safety. A major demerit of this approach is that the uncertainties in the material parameters, pore-water pressures, and loads due to earthquake are not in an explicit form in the factor of safety.

Slope stability analysis is important especially for different layered soils when it really becomes essential to determine the stability of the structure involved. For the designing of water conservancy structures like embankments, dams, etc the necessity parameter is stability number of the slope which was proposed by Taylor (1948). Many researchers and scientists provide the variation of stability numbers (N_s) (Taylor 1948; Chen 1975; Michalowksi 1994; 2002). Initially the most effective method to calculate stability number was the first-order second-moment method (FOSM). This method requires the performance function or its partial derivatives with respect to the basic random variables to be calculated at each iteration step.

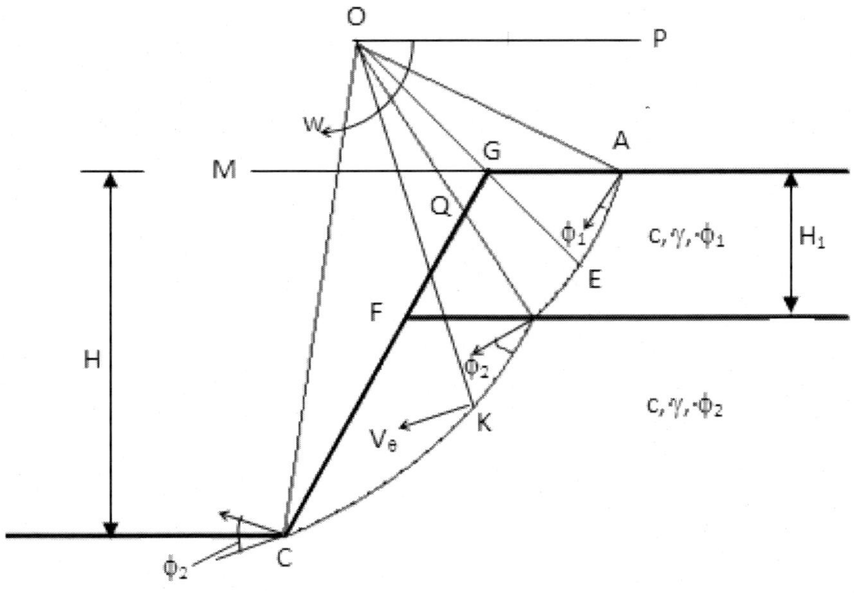

Figure 1. Slope geometry and collapse mechanism.

A large number of calculations of the performance function and its partial derivatives are therefore needed. Such calculations can be performed efficiently when the performance function can be expressed as an explicit form in terms of the basic variables. However, when the performance functions are implicit, such calculations require additional effort and may be time consuming. Conventional study is restricted to homogenous soil but this study makes use of four modelling techniques, Adaptive Neuro-Fuzzy Inference System (ANFIS), Gaussian Process Regression (GPR), Relevance Vector Machine (RVM), Extreme Learning Machine (ELM) applied to analyse slopes of different layered soil. The dataset have been collected from the work of Samui and Jyant (2006). The input data consists of slope angle(β), ratio of height of different layers (H_1/H_2), pore water pressure coefficient (r_u), horizontal earthquake acceleration coefficient(k_h), soil friction angles(φ_1 and φ_2) to find the stability number (N_s).

Adaptive Neuro-Fuzzy Inference System (ANFIS)

The model chosen was the Adaptive Neuro-Fuzzy Inference System or ANFIS, which is a representative of Sugeno- e -Tsukamoto fuzzy models. ANFIS gives an added advantage of combining the features of neural networks and fuzzy logic inference systems by Shahin et al. (2003). This means we obtain a powerful combination of the learning power of artificial neural networks and fuzzy logic system's explicit linguistic knowledge (Altrock 1995; Brown and Harris 1995).

Details of ANFIS

The fuzzy logic system of neurofuzzy networks store the knowledge acquired between a set of input variables $(x_1, x_2, ..., x_n)$ and the corresponding output variable y in a set of linguistic fuzzy rules that can be easily interpreted. Fuzzy logic system needs two main components to be determined. These are fuzzy sets and fuzzy rules. Fuzzy sets are determined by mathematically interpreting linguistic terms (e.g., small, medium, and large) in the form of membership functions, and fuzzifying model variables to behave as partial members of these membership functions in the interval grade (0,1). So, by transforming it into a degree of membership of the function $A(x)$ of interval (0,1) we can fuzzify an input variable x for a fuzzy set A. B-spline basis functions are piecewise polynomials of order k that can be used as one form of membership function.

In a process called fuzzification, the fuzzy sets overlap and cover the necessary range of variation for each variable. Defuzzification is required as the output is fuzzy in order to obtain a real-valued output. Although ANFIS utilizes an effective combination of several neural network features and fuzzy logic inference system, ANFIS faces gradient problems like a slow process speed and it may be trapped in local minima.

A neurofuzzy network typically comprises of three layers: an input layer; a single hidden layer; and an output layer. The input space is normalized in a p-dimensional lattice in which each cell of the lattice represents similar regions of the input space. The hidden layer contains the basis functions defined on the normalized input space. The complexity of the network structure is determined by the features of the basis function like size, shape and overlap.

Shahin et al., (2003) depicted that the output layer sums the weighted outputs from the basis functions to produce the network output using the following equation:

$$y = \sum_{i=1}^{p} = a_i w_i \qquad (1)$$

where y = model output; a_i = output from the pth basis function; and w_i = connection weight associated with a_i. After a comparison of the output generated through the equation and the actual measured output, the mean squared error MSE is calculated.

With this error and a learning rule, the weights and fuzzy parameters are decided by the neurofuzzy network.

In carrying out the formulation, the data has been branched into two sub-sets: such as

(a) A training dataset: This is required to construct the model. In this study, 1153 data are considered for training dataset.
(b) A testing dataset: This is required to evaluate the performance of the model. In this study, the remaining 288 data are considered as testing dataset.

GAUSSIAN PROCESS REGRESSION (GPR)

A Gaussian Process model can be called as a random process, with interconnected random variables subjected to a normal distribution. As stated earlier, it is entirely expressed in terms of mean and covariance. Gaussian distribution can be identified to be a collection of random variables $f(x_1),\ldots,f(x_n)N(0,\Sigma\ ),\Sigma x_p x_q$ $f(x_1),\ldots,f(x_n) \sim N(0,\Sigma)$, $\Sigma x_p x_q$ denotes the covariance existing between the cases p and q from the set of n-variables.

Details of GPR

If we consider a set of input variables $x_1, x_2,\ldots\ldots,x_n$ with a corresponding output variables $y_1, y_2,\ldots\ldots,y_n$ such that $y = f(x)$ then there exists a relationship such that $\mathrm{cov}(y_p, y_q) = C(x_p, x_q)$ which is a function with properties that generates a positive definite covariance matrix. This implies that the covariance between the output cases p and q is the same as that of the input variables. The covariance, therefore, depends upon the distance between the input space between x_p and x_q. Such a stationary attribute of the Gaussian Process Model helps one to use it for static non-linear system identification. The output obtained will have a higher smoothness with a higher covariance of x_p x_p and x_q x_q and a smaller Euclidian distance between the cases p and q.

For successful model identification a covariance function is to be wisely chosen and the most likely function used in this context is

$$C(x_p, x_q) = \vartheta \exp\left[(-0.5)\Sigma_{d=1}^{D} w_d \left(x_i^d - x_j^d\right)^2\right] + \delta_{ij}\vartheta_0 \qquad (2)$$

where D is the dimension of the input space vector X and the covariance function of the hyperparameters are determined by maximization of $p(f(X')/X,Y)$. Based on this, the value of $Y(N+1)$ can be determined as Y is dependent on X . $\theta = [w_1, w_2,\ldots.w_D, v_0, v_1]^T$ is the vector set of the hyper parameters of the input space which are to be determined with a set of training data.

The simplest type of Gaussian function (Azman and Kocijan 2007), where X is any input with y as an output with a share of noisy data, can be expressed as,

$$x(k) = f(x(k)) + \in(x) \tag{3}$$

where error function $\in(x) \sim N(0, K_{N+1})$ represents the white noise in the data collected. A successful model is one that minimizes this error function incurred. $x(k)$ represents the regressors, from the regressor input space, R^D being fed into the model with an attached hyperparameter. If a hyperparameter is closer or equal to zero, then the regressor will have a negligible or low impact on the output model.

Let us suppose a static system of an input space of dimension D, containing noisy data, such that $X = \lfloor X_1, X_2, ..., X_D \rfloor$ with an out vector data set $= [Y_1, Y_2, ..., Y_N]^T$. To approximate a distribution for an output $Y(N+1)$ due to a new input in the space $X' = [x_1(N+1), x_2(N+1), ..., x_D(N+1)]$ we have to first model a function dependent on both X and Y. Hence the model is structured on the basis of this function and not on fixed parameters. This quality helps in prediction of output without any control of the external conditions of the system.

For the collection of output variables, $Y = (Y_1, Y_2, ..., Y_{N+1})$ we can write by [3], $\begin{bmatrix} y \\ yN+1 \end{bmatrix} \sim N(0, K_{N+1})$ with covariance matrix,

$$K_{N+1} = \begin{bmatrix} [K] & [k(xN+1)] \\ [k(xN+1)T] & [x(x(N+1))] \end{bmatrix} \tag{4}$$

where $[Y_1, ..., Y_{N+1}]^T$ is an N*1 vector of training targets $k(x_{N+1}) = \lfloor c(X_1, X_{N+1}), ..., C(X_N, X_{N+1}) \rfloor^T$ is the N*1 vector of covariance between the training and test inputs, $k(x_{N+1}) = C(X_{N+1}, X_{N+1})$ is the auto covariance of the testing input.

To estimate the hyperparameters, $\theta = \left[w_1, w_2, \ldots w_D, v_0, v_1\right]^T$; where v_0 is the variance of the white noise in the training data set, the logarithmic function,

$$L(\theta) = \log(p(y \mid X)) = (-0.5)\log(|K|) - (0.5)y^T K^{-1} y - \left(\frac{N}{2}\right)\log(2\pi) \tag{5}$$

of the joint probability is maximized. Equation (5) is the logarithmic function with the vector parameters Θ and N*N covariance matrix K of the training data. To optimize this likelihood the partial derivative of the above equation is derived which is:

$$\frac{\partial L(\theta)}{\partial \theta i} = (-0.5)trace\left(K^{-1}\frac{\partial k}{\partial \theta i}\right) + (0.5)y^T K^{-1}\frac{\partial k}{\partial \theta_i}K^{-1}y \tag{6}$$

The above equation clearly indicates that calculation of the inverse matrix of *N***N* could become tedious whenever *N* is large. Now, as the parameters have been determined, we can obtain a GP model for $X(N+1)$ input. Hence the conditional probability gives an estimate of the output $Y(N+1)$ as,

$$p\left(y_{N+1} \mid y, X, x_{N+1}\right) = \frac{p(Y, YN+1)}{p(y \mid X)} \tag{7}$$

This is a Gaussian distribution with mean, $\mu\left(x_{N+1}\right) = k\left(x_{N+1}\right)^T K^{-1}$ and covariance $\sigma^2 = k\left(x_{N+1}\right) - k\left(x_{N+1}\right)^T K^{-1} k\left(x_{N+1}\right)$ (Azman and Kocijan 2007). Vector $k\left(x_{N+1}\right)^T K^{-1}$ is the vector which assigns the weights to Y, to make a prediction at the test point X(N+1). If the input is far away from the data points then $k\left(x_{N+1}\right)^T K^{-1} k\left(x_{N+1}\right)$ will be too small and hence variance will be large. This way identification of the type and quantity of data and white noise is determined with the help of variance. This model based on Gaussian Process Regression, when trained and tested for the normalised inputs, showed satisfactory results in compliance against the original data, with some amount of error. So, to overcome the shortcomings the data were further tested, this time with a combination of neuro-fuzzy inference system and neural network. In order to execute the GPR, the data has been divided into two sub-sets: such as

(a) A training dataset: This is required to construct the model. In this study, 1153 data are considered for training dataset.
(b) A testing dataset: This is required to evaluate the performance of the model. In this study, the remaining 288 data are considered as testing dataset.

RELEVANCE VECTOR MACHINE (RVM)

The important feature of the SVM is, its target function attempts to minimise a measure of error on the training set while simultaneously maximising the 'margin' between the two classes (in the feature space implicitly defined by the kernel). This is a highly effective mechanism for avoiding over-fitting (Tipping 2001). Despite of SVM's success in various fields, there are number of significant and practical demerits.

Relevance Vector Machine (RVM), developed by Tipping (2000) is a Bayesian form representing a generalized linear model of identical functional form of support vector machine (SVM). It differs with SVM in the case of solution which provides probabilistic interpretation of its outputs (Tipping 2000). This section describes a brief background of RVM technique. The complete description of RVM are available in Tipping (2000). Relevance vector machine (Tipping 2001) is simply a specialization of a spares Bayesian model which utilizes the same data dependent kernel basis. The key feature of RVM is that the inferred predictors are exceedingly sparse in that they contain relatively few "relevance vectors," as well as offering good generalization performance.

In RVM, a fully probabilistic framework is adopted and introduced a priori over the model weights governed by a set of hyperparameters, associated with weights, whose most probable values are iteratively estimated from the data. Sparsity is achieved because in practice the posterior distributions of many of the weights are sharply (indeed infinitely) peaked around zero. The remaining training vectors associated with non-zero weights are termed as relevance vectors.

Details of RVM

RVM starts with the concept of linear models, which are commonly used in a variety of regression problems, i.e., the function of y(x) needs to be predicted at some arbitrary point x given a set of (typically noisy) measurements of the function $t=(t_1,y, t_N)$ and some training points $x=(x_1,y, x_N)$:

$$t_i = y(x_i) + \varepsilon_i \tag{8}$$

where ε_i is the noise component of the measurement with mean 0 and variance σ^2. Under a linear model assumption, the unknown function y(x) is a linear combination of some known basis function i.e.

$$y(x) = \sum_{i=1}^{M} w_i \varphi_i(x) \tag{9}$$

where, $w=(w_1,\ldots,w_M)$ is a vector consisting of the linear combination weights and y(x) is the output is a linearly-weighted sum of M, generally nonlinear and fixed, basis functions $\varphi(x) = (\varphi_1(x), \varphi_2(x), \ldots\ldots\ldots\ldots, \varphi_M(x))^T$ Analysis of functions like is facilitated by Tipping (2001). Since the adjustable parameters (or 'weights') w appear linearly, and the objective is to estimate 'good' values for those parameters.

In this chapter, brief details and methodology of RVM is discussed i.e., the Bayesian probabilistic framework for learning the general models of the form was discussed. The key feature of this approach is it offers good generalisation performance; the inferred predictors are exceedingly sparse in that they contain relatively few non-zero weight parameters (w_i). The majority of parameters are automatically set to zero during the learning process, giving a procedure that is extremely effective at discerning those basis functions which are 'relevant' for making good predictions (Tipping 2000; 2001).

$$t = \Phi w + \varepsilon \tag{10}$$

where, Φ is an NxM design matrix, whose i^{th} column is formed with the values of basis function $\Phi_i(x)$ at all the training points, and $\varepsilon_i= (\varepsilon_1,\ldots, \varepsilon_N)$ is the noise vector. As a supervised learning, RVM starts with a set of data input $\{x_n\}_{n}^{N}=1$ and their corresponding target vector $\{t_n\}_{n}^{N}=1$. The aim of this 'training' set is to learn a model of the dependency of the target vectors on the inputs in order to make accurate prediction of *t* for previously unseen value of x. In the context of SVM, the prediction is estimated based on a function of the form

$$y(x)=\sum_{i=1}^{N} w_i K(x,x_i)+w_0 \tag{11}$$

where w= (w_1, w_2,..., w_N) is weight vectors, K(x,x_i) is a kernel function and $w_0$is the bias. In this study radial basis kernel function is used where the equation is as below

$$K(x_i,x)=\exp\left\{-\frac{(x_i-x)^T(x_i-x)}{2\sigma^2}\right\} \tag{12}$$

where, x_i and x are the training and test patterns, respectively, d is a dimension of the input vector and σ is width of the basis function.

Given a dataset of input-target pairs $\{x_n, t_n\}_{n}^{N}=1$, we follow the standard formulation and assume p(t|x) is Gaussian N(t|y(x),σ^2). The mean of this distribution for a given x is modelled by y(x) as defined in Eq.(11). The likelihood of dataset can be written as

$$p(t|w,\sigma^2)=\left(2\pi\sigma^2\right)^{-N/2}\exp\left\{-\frac{1}{2\sigma^2}\|t-\Phi w\|^2\right\} \tag{13}$$

where, $t_i=(t_1...,t_N)^T$, $\omega_i=(\omega_0,...,\omega_N)$ and

$$\Phi^T=\begin{bmatrix}1 & K(x_1,x_1) & K(x_1,x_2) & \cdots & K(x_1,x_n)\\ 1 & K(x_2,x_1) & K(x_2,x_2) & \cdots & K(x_2,x_n)\\ \vdots & \vdots & \vdots & \vdots & \vdots\\ 1 & K(x_n,x_1) & K(x_n,x_2) & \cdots & K(x_n,x_n)\end{bmatrix}$$

where, $k(x_i, x_n)$ is a kernel function. Maximum likelihood estimation of w and σ^2 in equation (13) often results in overfitting. Therefore, Tipping (2001) recommended imposition of some prior constrains on the parameters w by adding a complexity to the likelihood or error function. This is a priori information controls the generalization ability of the learning process. Typically, new higher-level parameters are used to constrain an explicit zero-mean Gaussian prior probability distribution over the weights

$$p(w|\alpha) = \prod_{i=0}^{N} N\left(w_i|0, \alpha_i^{-1}\right) \tag{14}$$

where α is a vector of (N+1) hyperparameters that controls how far from zero each weights is allowed to deviate (Caesarendra et al. 2010). Using Bayes' rule, the posterior over all unknowns could be computed, given the defined non-informative prior-distributions. To complete the specification of the prior-distribution, one must define hyperpriors over α and noise variance σ^2. These quantities are examples of scale parameters and suitable prior are Gamma Distributions (Tipping 2000)

$$p(\alpha) = \prod_{i=0}^{N} Gamma(\alpha_i|a, b), \tag{15}$$

$$p(\beta) = \prod_{i=0}^{N} Gamma(\beta|c, d) \tag{16}$$

where, $\beta = \sigma^{-2}$. Thus, for α and σ it is gamma distribution and for w it is normal distribution and after the prior-distributions, Bayes rule is applied.

$$p\left(w, \alpha, \sigma^2|t\right) = \frac{p\left(t|w, \alpha, \sigma^2\right)p\left(w, \alpha, \sigma^2\right)}{p(t)} \tag{17}$$

Then, given a new test point (X_*), predictions are made for the corresponding target (t_*), in terms of the predictive distribution:

$$p(t_*|t) = \int p\left(t_*|w, \alpha, \sigma^2\right)p\left(w, \alpha, \sigma^2|t\right) dw\, d\alpha\, d\sigma^2 \tag{18}$$

However, computing the solution of the posterior in equation (18) directly is not possible, since we cannot perform the normalizing integral $p(t) = \int p\left(t \middle| w, \alpha, \sigma^2\right) p\left(w, \alpha, \sigma^2 \middle| t\right) dw\ d\alpha\ d\sigma^2$. Instead, we decompose the posterior as in equation (19)

$$p\left(w, \alpha, \sigma^2 \middle| t\right) = p\left(w \middle| t, \alpha, \sigma^2\right) p\left(\alpha, \sigma^2 \middle| t\right) \tag{19}$$

It should be noted that one can compute analytically the posterior distribution over the weights since its normalization integral is convolution of Gaussians (Tipping, 2000). Thus, to facilitate the solution. The posterior distribution of weights is given by

$$p\left(w \middle| t, \alpha, \sigma^2\right) = \frac{p\left(t \middle| w, \sigma^2\right) p(w, \alpha)}{p(t | \alpha, \sigma^2)} \tag{20}$$

Thus, the posterior over the weights is then obtained from Bayes'rule

$$p\left(w \middle| t, \alpha, \sigma^2\right) = (2\pi)^{-(N+1)/2} |\Sigma|^{-1/2} \exp\left\{-\frac{1}{2}(w-\mu)^T \Sigma^{-1} (w-\mu)\right\} \tag{21}$$

Equation (21) has an analytical solution where the posterior covariance and mean are

$$\Sigma = \left(\sigma^{-2} \Phi^T \Phi + A\right)^{-1} \tag{22}$$

$$\mu = \sigma^{-2} \Sigma \Phi^T t \tag{23}$$

where we have defined A = (α_0, $\alpha_{1\ldots}$ α_N). Note that σ^2 is also treated as a hyperparameter, which may be estimated from the data. Therefore, machine learning becomes a search for the hyperparameters posterior most probable, i.e., maximization of $p\left(\alpha, \alpha^2_{\in_n} \middle| y\right) \alpha p\left(y \middle| \alpha, \alpha^2_{\in_n}\right) p(\alpha) p\left(\alpha^2_{\in_n}\right)$ with respect to a α

and σ^2. For uniform hyperpriors, it is required to maximize the term $p\left(y|\alpha, \alpha_{\in_n}^2\right)$, which is computed and given by

$$p\left(y|\alpha, \alpha_{\in_n}^2\right) = \int p\left(y|w, \alpha_{\in_n}^2\right) p(w|\alpha) dw$$
$$= (2\pi)^{-1/2} \left|\alpha_{\in_n}^2 I + \Phi A^{-1} \Phi^T\right|^{1/2}$$
$$\times \exp\left\{-\frac{1}{2} y^T \left(\alpha_{\in_n}^2 I + \Phi A^{-1} \Phi^T|\right)^{-1} y\right\} \tag{24}$$

Tipping (2000) arrived this approximation and found that, all the evidence from several experiments suggests that this approximation is very effective. Bayesian models refer to equation (16) as the marginal likelihood, and its maximization is known as the type II-maximum likelihood method (Ghosh and Mujumdar 2008). Tipping (2000) refers this as the evidence for hyperparameter and its maximization as the evidence procedure. Hyperparameter estimation is typically carried out with an iterative formula such as a gradient ascent on the objective function (Tipping 2000; Ghosh and Mujumdar 2008). Predictions for a new data are then made according to integration of the weights to obtain the marginal likelihood for the hyperparameters. The predictive distribution for a given input vector, {x} can be computed using following equation. The predictions are made based on the posterior distribution over the weights, conditioned on the maximized most probable values of α and $\sigma_{\in_n}^2$, α_{MP} and σ_{MP}^2 respectively.

$$p\left(y_*|y, \alpha_{MP}, \sigma_{MP}^2\right) = \int p\left(y_*|w, \sigma_{MP}^2\right) p\left(w|y, \alpha_{MP}, |\sigma_{MP}^2\right) dw \tag{25}$$

This can be readily computed given that,

$$p\left(y_*|y, \alpha_{MP}, \sigma_{MP}^2\right) = N\left(y_*|t_*, \sigma_*^2\right) \tag{26}$$

$$t_* = \mu^T \Phi(x_*) \tag{27}$$

With

$$\sigma_*^2 = \sigma_{MP}^2 + \Phi(x_*)^T \Sigma \Phi(x_*) \tag{28}$$

the outcome of the optimization involved in RVM (i.e., max of $p\left(y \middle| \alpha, \sigma_{\epsilon_n}^2\right)$), is that many of α go to infinity such that w will have only a few nonzero weights that will be considered as relevant vectors (Ghosh and Mujumdar, 2008). The relevant vectors (RVs) can be viewed as counterparts of support vectors (SVs) in SVM. thus, the developed model contains the benefits of SVM (sparsity and generalization) and in addition, provides estimates of uncertainty bounds in the predictions they make (Ghosh and Mujumdar 2008). Same dataset segregation as that of ANFIS and GPR, RVM also have been adopted to develop the model.

EXTREME LEARNING MACHINE (ELM)

The learning rate in conventional artificial learning methodology is slow since the input weights are tuned iteratively to attain high performance with local minima. The architecture of extreme machine learning is constructed in such a way that it works as the functioning of the brain and the system is trained without the process of iteration. This structure overcomes the constraint of traditional learning techniques by integrating the concept of neural network, concept of matrix, linear algebra for generalization with randomness. The ELM performs fast and has good generalization ability. Itis a potential robust method for approaching complex, non-linear problems in geotechnical engineering.

Details of ELM

Extreme learning machine is a simple computation technique to train the system and this unifies the methodology of traditional neural network of single layer feedforward neural network to enhance the performance in the real time applications by overcoming the limitations of FFNN. Single layer feedforward network has an ability to run all the applications which consists of series of inputs and outputs with the interconnection of neurons whereby each neuron calculate the activation function with the given inputs, weights and the bias which approximates the function of any continuous targeted function or any disjoint region by tuning the parameters. ELMs have both universal approximation and classification capabilities; they also build a direct link between multiple theories (specifically, ridge regression, optimization, neural network generalization performance, linear system stability, and matrix theory).

Most popularly used method is gradient descent-based method of feed-forward neural network. Gradient descent-based method and RBF is popularly used method in neural network where the ouput of the network with respect to the input (X_i)to the target output(t_j) is not exactly the same, and hence some error is retrieved with the output say(O_j). Hence this function has to be minimized, so in order to minimize the function researchers spend time for finding the different methods of how to tune the hidden layer parameters(a_i, b_i)and mostly in all the networks so many parameters has to be tuned with N number of hidden nodes with the limitations of local minima, slow learning rate, human interventions. To find a solution or to optimize and minimize this problem Kernel based method was proposed called Support vector machine is introduced. ELM has unified all these approach by improving the learning speed, obtaining negligible error by analytically determining the parameters without any iterative tuning process and this system with the consideration of linearity it formulates the solution using Moore-Penrose generalized pseudo inverse to achieve a better performance of generalization and least square method is used to reach the best fit solution incorporated with the minimum norm.

The architecture of extreme learning machine is based on the structure of single-hidden layer feedforward neural networks (SLFNs) which comprises of three layers of interconnecting neurons from Input layer to Hidden layer and weights from hidden to Output Layer. Single-hidden layer feedforward neural networks are trained with L hidden neuron with N random sample input sets (x_i, t_i) where x_i is the input given to the system and t_i is the targeted function (Huang et al. 2006).

$$x_i = \left[x_{i1}, x_{i2} \ldots\ldots\ldots, x_{n-1}, x_n\right]^T \in R^n \tag{29}$$

$$t_i = \left[t_{i1}, t_{i2} \ldots\ldots\ldots, t_{m-1}, t_m\right]^T \in R^m \tag{30}$$

Generally tuning in hidden layer is not required in extreme learning machine where all the parameters in the hidden layer are randomly generated and hidden nodes can be of infinity in number or fixed N number of nodes Output from input layer neurons in the structure is approximated by an activation function g(x) of each instances, there are various activation function among them sigmoid function is the mostly used function and it can be balanced between linear and nonlinear parameters which is derived as a S-shaped graph.

$$g(x) = \sum_{i=1} \alpha i \, g_i(X_j) \tag{31}$$

$$g(x) = \sum_{i=1}^{L} \alpha_i g_i(w_i . x_i + b_i) = Z_j \quad \{i = 1 \ldots\ldots\ldots N\} \tag{32}$$

In the above mentioned equation $w_i = \lfloor w_{i1}, w_{i2} \ldots\ldots, w_{n-1}, w_n \rfloor^T$ is the Weight vector that is Connected between input layer and hidden layer of each neurons in the layer. αi= [αi1, $\alpha_i = \lfloor \alpha_{i1}, \alpha_{i2} \ldots\ldots, \alpha_{m-1}, \alpha_m \rfloor^T$. Weight vector that is connected from Hidden layer to output layer with the interconnection of every instances. b_i is the Threshold of Bias of the each ith neuron in the hidden layer. There are various activation function say, Fourier function, Gaussian function, Multiquadrics function etc (Huang et al. 2015) but most commonly used is Sigmoid function g(x) which approximate the random weights and input samples to zero error such that the output matrix matches the targeted value that has to be reached.

While training the system negligible amount of training error is obtained with the probability one when the numbers of hidden nodes are equal to training datasets. In other cases if the number of hidden nodes are equal to the number of datasets then the training error leads to zero

$$g(x) = \sum_{i=1}^{L} \| O_j - t_j \| = 0 \tag{33}$$

$$g(X) = \sum_{i=1}^{L} \alpha_i g(W_i \cdot X_i + b_i) = t_j \tag{34}$$

$$g(x)=\sum_{i=1}\alpha_i g(w_i.x_i+b_i)=t_j \qquad \{j=1,.....,N\} \tag{35}$$

The Non-Linear system has been modified to linear system whereby the above equation can be briefly written precisely as

$$H\alpha=T \tag{36}$$

where H is the Output matrix of the hidden layer with respective inputs xi, α is the Output weight matrix, T is the Target matrix.

Equation (36) can be written as:

$$H(w_{i1},....,w_l,b_1...b_l,x_1....x_l)=\begin{pmatrix} g(w_1.x_1+b_1).....g(w_l.x_1+b_L) \\ \vdots \quad .... \quad \vdots \\ \vdots \quad .... \quad \vdots \\ g(w_1.x_1+b_1).....g(w_l.x_1+b_L) \end{pmatrix}_{NxL} \tag{37}$$

$$\alpha=\begin{pmatrix} \alpha_1^t \\ \vdots \\ \vdots \\ \vdots \\ \alpha_L^t \end{pmatrix}_{Lxm} \text{ and } \quad T=\begin{pmatrix} t_1^t \\ \vdots \\ \vdots \\ \vdots \\ t_l^t \end{pmatrix}_{Lxm}$$

As the equation {Hα=T} satisfies the linear equation Ax = y with the set of [mxn] matrix. If m=n, y represent column vector then unique Solution is determined where A has an inverse $x = A^{-1}y$. The product of the matrix and its inverse gives identity matrix when the matrix is of square. In real time applications the matrix may be or may not be square matrix and hence generalize inverse is used for the rectangular matrix which is called as pseudo inverse matrix.

To get hold of optimization or linear system problems and to generalize the solution inverse matrix solution Moore-Penrose pseudo-inverse solution used minimum norm of least square solution with the equation $\alpha=H^{\dagger}T$, denotes the Moore-Penrose pseudo-inverse which is a unique matrix that satisfy the below mentioned properties (Barata and Hussein 2012).

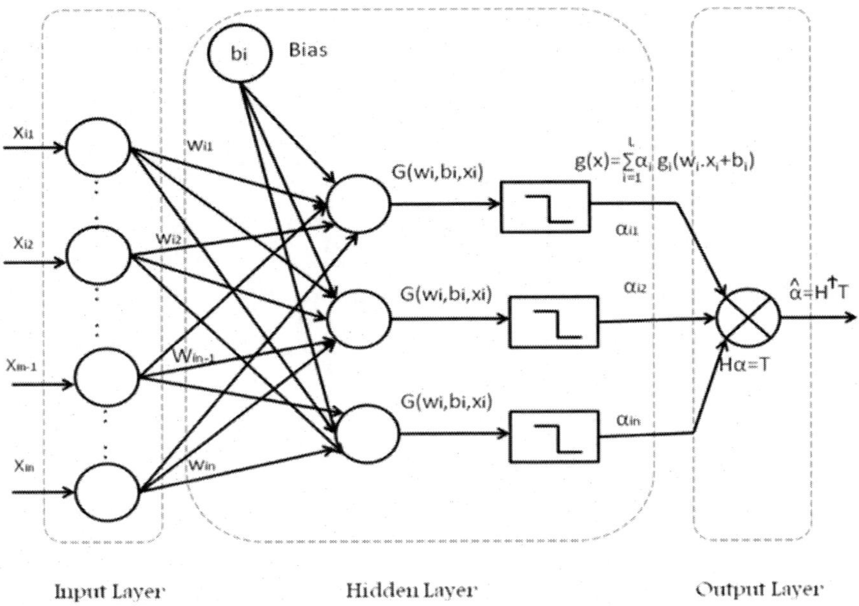

Figure 2. Architecture of ELM.

- H H† H = H
- H† H H† = H†
- (H H†) T = H H†
- (H† H) T = H† H

If the output matrix matches the first two conditions then it is a weak generalized inverse. And if the matrix equals the third condition then it is normalized generalized inverse.

And the first and fifth constrain is satisfied then minimum norm generalized inverse.

By computing the linear system to minimum quadratic solution is $\hat{\alpha} = H^{+}T$ In case when m<n then the solution obtained may or may not be unique whereby the Euclidean norm which means Least squares method is used to approximate the solution to obtain the smallest possible value which is called as minimizing set of vectors $\| Ax^{1} - y \|$.

$\hat{\alpha} = Min \| H\alpha = T \|$ [Training error is minimized]

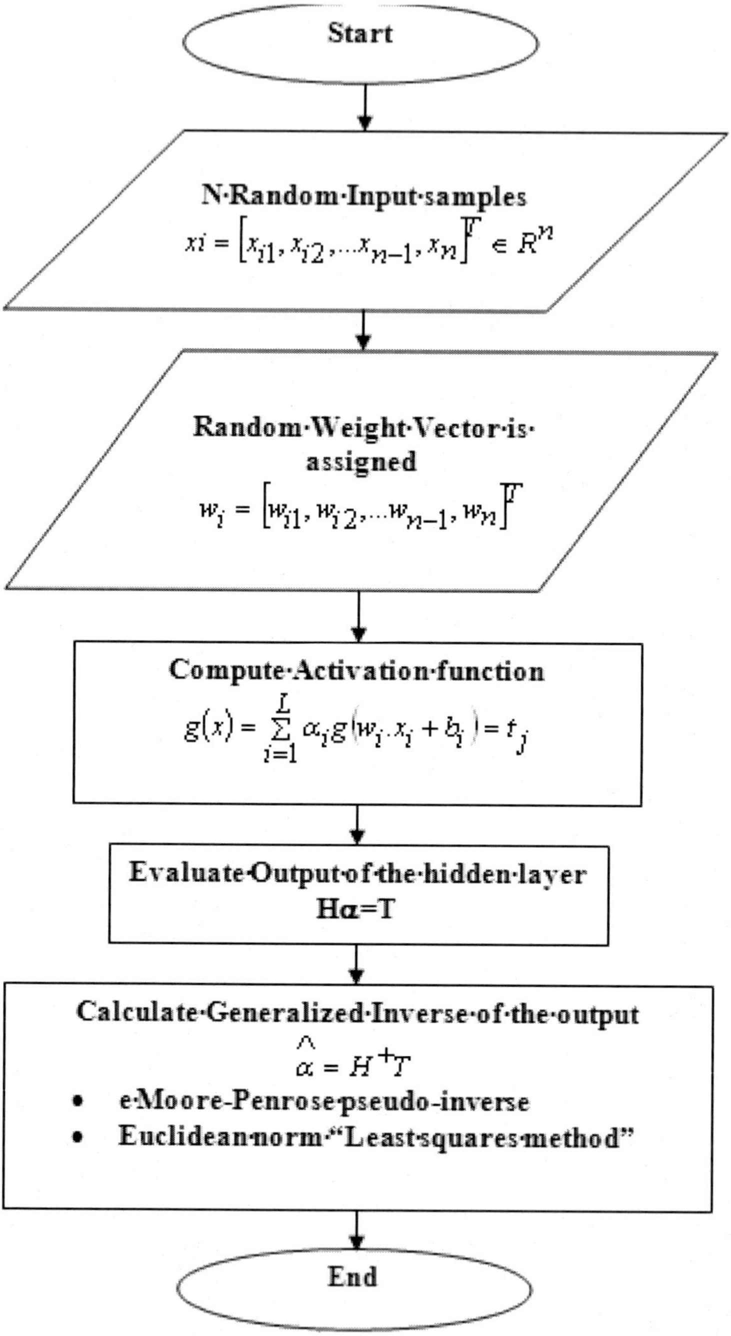

Figure 3. Flowchart shows the procedure of ELM.

$\| \alpha \| = \| H + T \| \leq \| \alpha \|$ [Approximated to least possible value by Euclidean norm or Magnitude of the system corresponding to the orthogonal projection of vector space].

The following flow chart reveals the technical procedure ELM. ELM adopts the same dataset used for the above mentioned models.

RESULTS AND DISCUSSIONS

In ANFIS model, the hypothesized initial numbers of membership functions for each input are 17. A suitable pattern has to be chosen for the best performance of the network.

After the training (with 70 epochs) was complete, the final configuration for the Fuzzy Inference System (FIS) is:

Number of output membership functions=17

Number of fuzzy rules=17

Neuro-fuzzy adaptive network for N_s

1. Number of input=6
2. Number of membership function for each input=17
3. Type of membership functions for each input= Gaussian
4. Type of membership functions for each output= Linear
5. Number of training epochs = 70
6. Training performance(R) = 0.853
7. Testing performance(R) = 0.8181

The performance of the developed ANFIS model can be assessed in terms of coefficient of correlation (R). For a good model, the value of R should be greater than 0.8 (Smith 1986).

The following Figure 4 shows the performance of ANFIS model in terms of R.

The design values of ε and width (s) of radial basis function can be obtained by trial and error approach. The constructed GPR model provide the best performance at ε = 1.9 and s = 0.85.

The performance of the developed GPR model can be assessed in terms of coefficient of correlation (R). Smith (1986) declares that for a better model the R value should be greater than 0.8. The following Figure 5 depicts the performance of GPR model in terms of R.

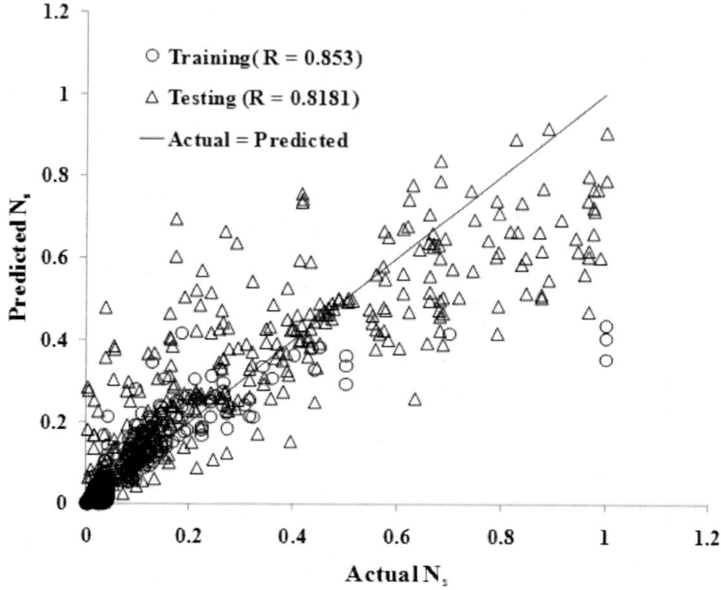

Figure 4. Performance of the developed ANFIS model.

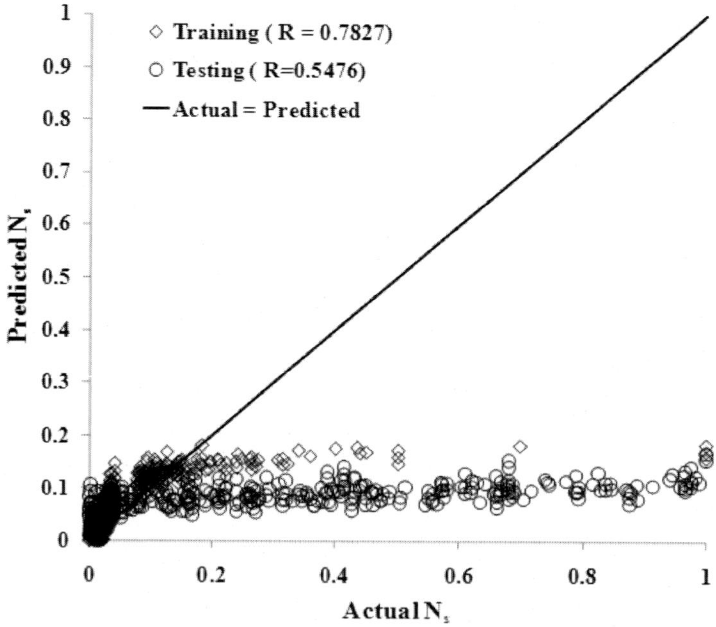

Figure 5. Performance of the developed GPR model.

The developed RVM gives the following equation for prediction of liquefaction susceptibility of soil.

$$N_s = \left(\sum_{i=1}^{1152} w_i \exp\left\{ -\frac{(x_i - x)(x_i - x)^T}{5810.42} \right\} \right) \tag{38}$$

In order to find out the Ns, the above equation can be used, which w value can be determined from the following Figure 6.

The developed RVM performance can be assessed by the performance of R value. The following Figure 7 reveals the performance of the developed RVM model. For the ELM model, best performance is obtained at 12 hidden nodes.

Therefore, the number of hidden nodes is set to 12. Radial basis function has been adopted as radial basis function. Figure 8 depicts the performance of ELM respectively. As shown in Figures 8, the value of R is close to one for training as well as testing datasets.

The developed models have been compared based on the coefficient of correlation (R) value. The following Figure 9 conveyed that the developed ELM is superior to the other developed models.

For developing the ANFIS model three tuning parameters have been considered, whereas for GPR two tuning parameters are considered, however ELM and RVM considered only one.

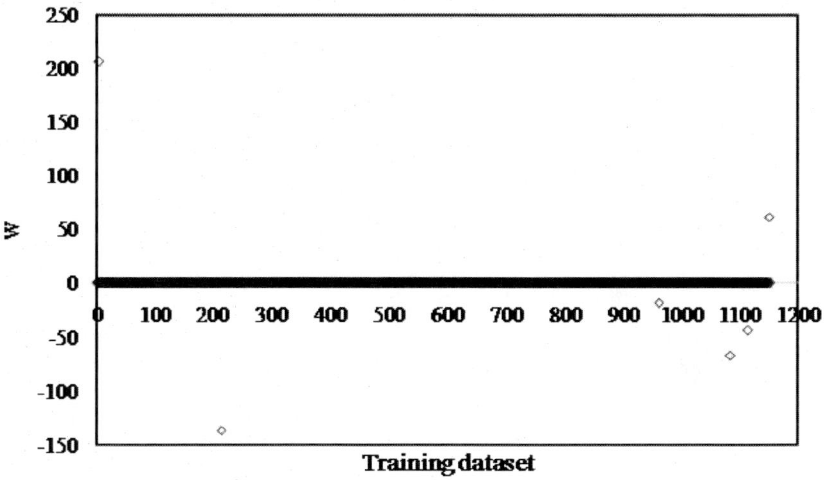

Figure 6. Values of w.

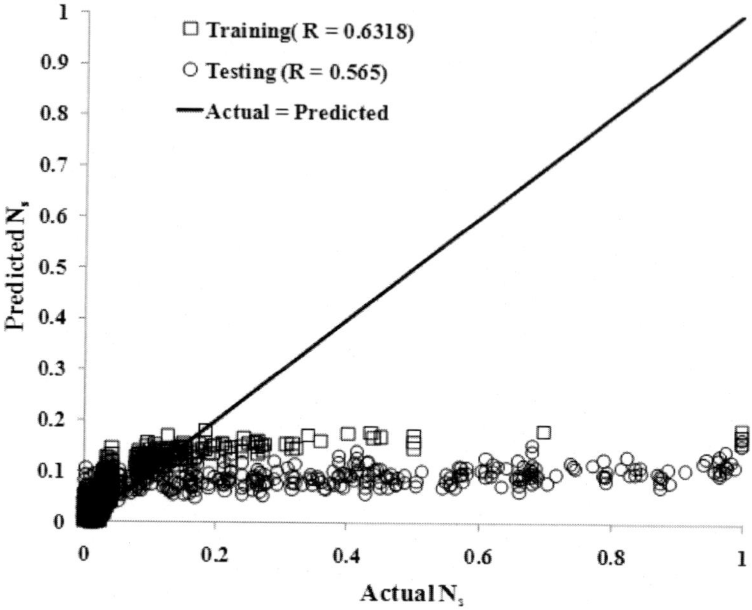

Figure 7. Performance of the developed RVM model.

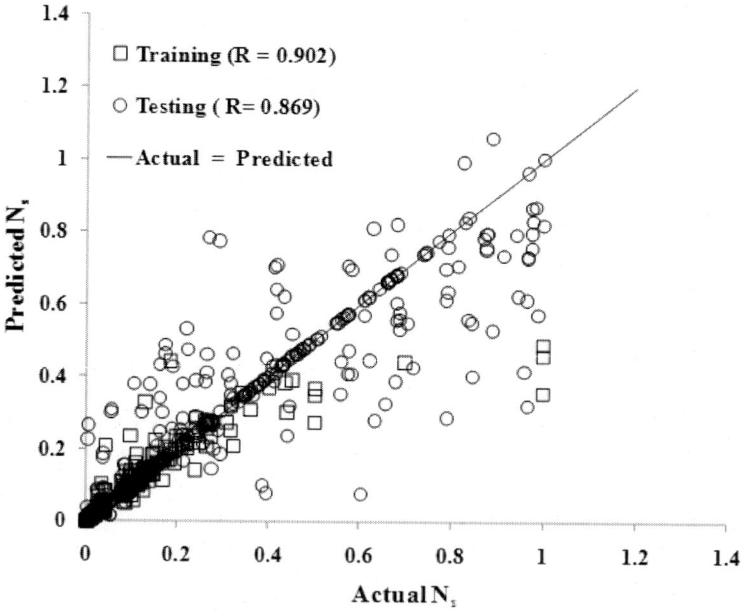

Figure 8. Performance of the developed ELM model.

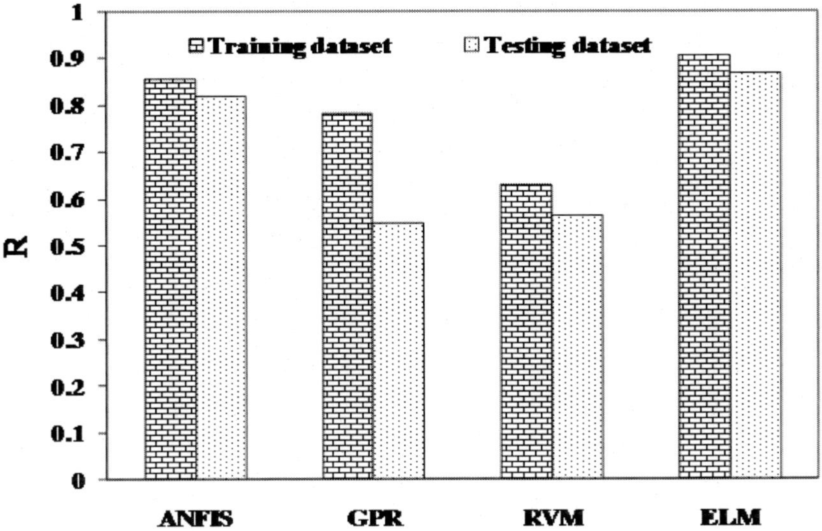

Figure 9. Comparison of the developed models.

The developed models can also be justified by the statistical performances.

In the present study different statistical parameters have been employed for judging the actual and predicted stability number. The parameters include: Root Mean Square Error (RMSE), Mean Absolute Percentage Error (MAPE), Coefficient of Corelation (R), Coefficient of Efficiency (E), Root Mean Square Error to observation's standard deviation ratio (RSR) and Normalized Mean Bias Error (NMBE). The developed model statistical performances were determined and evaluated by using the following equations (Vinay et al. 2015).

$$MAPE = \frac{\sum_{i=1}^{n} \left| h_i - t_i \right|}{n} \tag{39}$$

$$RMSE = \sqrt{\frac{\sum_{i=1}^{n} \left(h_i - t_i \right)^2}{n}} \tag{40}$$

$$R = \frac{\sum_{i=1}^{n}\left(h_i - \bar{h}_i\right)\left(t_i - \bar{t}_i\right)}{\sqrt{\sum_{i=1}^{n}\left(h_i - \bar{h}_i\right)^2 \sum_{i=1}^{n}\left(t_i - \bar{t}_i\right)^2}} \quad (41)$$

$$E = 1 - \frac{\sum_{i=1}^{N}\left(h_i - t_i\right)^2}{\sum_{i=1}^{N}\left(h_i - \bar{h}_i\right)^2} \quad (42)$$

$$RSR = \frac{RMSE}{\sqrt{\frac{1}{N}\sum_{i=1}^{N}\left(h_i - \bar{h}_i\right)^2}} \quad (43)$$

$$NMBE(\%) = \frac{\frac{1}{N}\sum_{i=1}^{N}\left(t_i - h_i\right)}{\frac{1}{N}\sum_{i=1}^{N} h_i} \text{x}\,100 \quad (44)$$

where h_i and t_i are respectively the measured and predicted Ns values, $\bar{h}_i$ and $\bar{t}_i$ are the average of the measured and predicted outputs, and n is the total number of dataset. The following tables reveal the statistical performances of the various developed models.

Table 1. Statistical performances of the developed models for the training dataset

	ANFIS	**GPR**	**RVM**	**ELM**
MAPE (%)	22.197	71.91	71.90	8.987
RMSE	7.407	10.98	10.98	6.438
E	0.726	-0.664	-0.664	0.7556
RSR	0.523	0.774	0.774	0.494
NMBE	0.104	-0.0064	-0.0064	-0.528

Table 2. Statistical performances of the developed models for the testing dataset

	ANFIS	GPR	RVM	ELM
MAPE(%)	6.567	15.347	15.34	3.925
RMSE	1.083	2.668	2.668	0.927
E	0.666	-1.02	-1.023	0.7556
RSR	0.577	1.422	1.422	0.494
NMBE	0.098	-16.38	-5.105	-0.528

The above tables convey the comparison of statistical performances of different developed models.

CONCLUSION

This chapter discuss the efficiency of soft computing techniques like ANFIS, GPR, RVM and ELM, in predicting the stability number of the layered slope. The technical procedures of the above mentioned techniques have been executed accordingly and proved their capability on determining the N_s value. From the above mentioned developed models, ELM outperforms the other models with an elegant and encouraging performance. Hence, these impressive models can be used in various arduous problems of geotechnical engineering.

REFERENCES

Altrock, C. V. (1995). Fuzzy logic and neurofuzzy applications explained. New Jersey, Prentice-Hall.

Azman, K., and Kocijan, J. (2007). Application of Gaussian Processes for Black-Box Modelling Systems. *ISA Trans., 46*(4), 443 - 57.

Barata1, J. C. A., and Hussein, M. S. (2012). The Moore-Penrose Pseudoinverse. A Tutorial Review of the Theory. *Brazilian Journal of Physics, 42*(1-2), 146-165.

Brown, M., and Harris, C. (1994). Neurofuzzy adaptive modeling and control. New Jersey, Prentice-Hall.

Caesarendraa, W., Achmad, W., and Yang, B. S. (2010). Application of relevance vector machine and logistic regression for machine degradation assessment. *Mechanical Systems and Signal Processing, 24*(4), 1161–1171.

Chandwani, V., Agrawal, V., and Ravindra, N. (2015). Modeling slump of ready mix concrete using genetic algorithms assisted training of Artificial Neural Networks. *Expert Systems with Applications, 42*, 885 – 893.

Chen, W. F. (1975). Limit analysis and soil plasticity. Amsterdam, Elsevier.

Gao, H., Guang, B. H., Shiji, S., Keyou, Y. (2015). Trends in extreme learning machines: A review. *Neural Networks, 61*, 32 – 48.

Ghosh, S., and Mujumdar, P. P. (2008). Statistical downscaling of GCM simulations to streamflow using relevance vector machine. *Advances in Water Resources, 31*, 132 – 146.

Huang, G. B., Zhu, Q. Y., and Siew, C. K. (2006). Extreme learning machine: Theory and applications. *Neurocomputing, 70*(1–3), 489 – 501.

Jyant, K., and Samui, P. (2006). Stability determination for layered soil slopes using the upper bound limit analysis. *Geotechnical and Geological Engineering Journal, 24*(6), 1803 - 1819.

Michalowski, R. L. (2002). Stability charts for uniform slopes. *Journal of Geotechnical and Geoenvirometal Engineering, ASCE, 128*(4), 351 - 355.

Michalowski, R. L. (1994). Limit analysis of slopes subjected to pore pressure. In Srirwardane and Zaman (Eds.), Proceeding, Conference on Comp. Methods and Advances in Geomechanics. Balkema, Rotterdam, The Netherlands.

Shahin, M. A., Jaksa, M. B., and Maier, H. R. (2003). Neurofuzzy networks applied to settlement of shallow foundations on granular soils. In D. K. Madanat and Pestana (Eds.), Applications of Statistics and Probability in Civil Engineering. Rotterdam: Millpress.

Smith, G. N. (1986). Probability and Statistics in Civil Engineering. London, Collins.

Taylor, D. W. (1948). Fundamental of soil mechanics. New York, John Wiley.

Tipping, M. E. (2000). The relevance vector machine. *Advances in Neural Information Processing Systems, 12*, 625 - 658.

Tipping, M. E. (2001). Sparse Bayesian learning and the relevance vector machine. *Journal of Machine Learning Research, 1*, 211 – 244.

ADDITIONAL READING SECTION

Ahmad, M., and Nasser L. A. (2014). Optimally pruned extreme learning machine with ensemble of regularization techniques and negative correlation penalty applied to automotive engine coldstart hydrocarbon emission identification. *Neurocomputing, 131*, 143-156.

Ahmad, M., and Nasser L. A. (2014). Optimally pruned extreme learning machine with ensemble of regularization techniques and negative correlation penalty applied to automotive engine coldstart hydrocarbon emission identification. *Neurocomputing, 131*, 143-156.

Audrey, V., Maxime, B., Roland, H., Gustave, M., André, L., and Steven, L. (2011). Relevance vector machine consciousness classifier applied to cerebral metabolism of vegetative and locked-in patients. *NeuroImage, 56*(2), 797–808.

Cernuschi, F., Bruno, R., and John, D. (1988). On the exact maximum like lihood estimation of gaussian autoregressive processes. *IEEE Transactions on Acoustics, Speech, and Signal Processing, 36*(6), 922 - 929.

Debby, D. W., Ran, W., and Hong, Y. (2014). Fast prediction of protein–protein interaction sites based on Extreme Learning Machines. *Neurocomputing, 128*, 258 - 266.

Engin, A. (2013). A new method for expert target recognition system: Genetic wavelet extreme learning machine (GAWELM). *Expert Systems with Applications, 40*(10), 3984 - 3993.

Escandell Montero, P., Martínez Martínez, J. M., Martín Guerrero, J. D., Soria Olivas, E., Gómez Sanchis, J. (2014). Least-squares temporal difference learning based on an extreme learning machine. *Neurocomputing, 141*, 37 - 45.

Fei, H., Hai Fen, Y., Qing Hua, L. (2013). An improved evolutionary extreme learning machine based on particle swarm optimization. *Neurocomputing, 116*, 87 - 93.

Felix S. F., Renan, A. A., Elmer, C. R., William, E. H., Rubens, M. F., and Luiz, P. L. (2014). Product Quality Monitoring Using Extreme Learning Machines and Bat algorithms: A Case Study in Second-Generation Ethanol Production. *Computer Aided Chemical Engineering, 33*, 955 - 960.

Frénay, B., Mark van, H., Yoan, M., Michel, V., and Amaury, L. (2013). Feature selection for nonlinear models with extreme learning machines. *Neurocomputing, 102*, 111 - 124.

Girolami, M., and Rogers, S. (2006). Variational Bayesian multinomial probit regression with gaussian process priors. *Neural Computation, 18*(8), 1790-1817.

Guohu, L., Min, L., and Dong, M. (2010). A new online learning algorithm for structure-adjustable extreme learning machine. *Computers and Mathematics with Applications, 60*(3), 377 - 389.

Guoqiang, L., Peifeng, N., Yunpeng, M., Hongbin, W., and Weiping, Z. (2014). Tuning extreme learning machine by an improved artificial bee colony to model and optimize the boiler efficiency. *Knowledge-Based Systems, 67*, 278 - 289.

Heyns, T., De Villiers, J. P., and Heyns, P. S. (2012). Consistent haul road condition monitoring by means of vehicle response normalisation with Gaussian processes. *Engineering Applications of Artificial Intelligence, 25*(8), 1752 - 1760.

Hongming, Y., Jun, Y., Junhua, Z., ZhaoYang, D. (2013). Extreme learning machine based genetic algorithm and its application in power system economic dispatch. *Neurocomputing, 102*, 154 - 162.

Jeffrey, P., and Nalini, R. (2009). Maximum likelihood estimation in vector long memory processes via EM algorithm. *Computational Statistics and Data Analysis, 53*(12), 4133 - 4142.

Lebarbier, E. (2005). Detecting multiple change-points in the mean of gaussian process by model selection. *Signal Processing, 85*(4), 717 - 736.

Shi, J. Q., Murray Smith, R., and Titterington, D. M. (2003). Bayesian regression and classification using mixtures of gaussian processes. *International Journal of Adaptive Control and Signal Processing, 17*(2), 149 - 161.

Sundararajan, S., and Keerthi, S. S. (2001). Predictive approaches for choosing hyperparameters in gaussian processes. *Neural Computation, 13*(5), 1103-1118.

Van Gestel, T., Suykens, J. A. K., Lanckriet, G., Lambrechts, A., De Moor, B., and Vandewalle, J. (2002). Bayesian framework for least-squares support vector machine classifiers, gaussian processes, and kernel fisher discriminant analysis. *Neural Computation, 14*(5), 1115 - 1147.

Yuan, J., Wang, K., Yu, T., and Fang, M. (2008). Reliable multi-objective optimization of high-speed WEDM process based on Gaussian process regression. *International Journal of Machine Tools and Manufacture, 48*(1), 47 - 60.

In: Soft Computing
Editor: Alan Casey
ISBN: 978-1-63485-133-6

Chapter 3

MULTILAYER WAVELET-NEURO-FUZZY SYSTEMS IN DYNAMIC DATA MINING TASKS

***Yevgeniy Bodyanskiy*[1,*]*, Olena Vynokurova*[1]*, Iryna Pliss*[1]
***and Pavlo Mulesa*[2]
[1]Kharkiv National University of Radio Electronics, Kharkiv, Ukraine
[2]Uzghorod National Univesity, Uzghorod, Ukraine

ABSTRACT

This book chapter is devoted the intensive developing in our days Soft Computing systems especially Wavelet-Neuro-Fuzzy Systems (WNFS) in Dynamic Data Mining tasks, when the data are fed sequentially to the processing in on-line mode. Although the many type of such hybrid systems and their learning algorithms are known by now, but all of them can operate only in batch mode, when all data sample is defined a priori.

The advantages of WNFS are universal approximation properties and learning abilities, which reside in the artificial neural networks, results transparency and interpretability, which reside in the fuzzy inference systems, possibility of the local features signal analysis, which reside in the wavelet systems. The additional flexibility of considered systems is provided by using the specialized adaptive learning algorithms allowed to tune in on-line mode both the synaptic weights and activation-membership functions parameters and the shape of these functions and also the architectures of the synthesized system.

[*] Corresponding author: yevgeniy.bodyanskiy@nure.ua.

As the nodes of multilayer WNFS the neo-fuzzy-neuron and the wavelet neuron (which was synthesized based on neo-fuzzy neuron) with adaptive membership functions that can change their shape in learning process from the conventional Gaussian to even function of wavelet «Maxican Hat» are considered.

The modification of Levenberg-Marquardt learning algorithm for the tuning of all nodes' parameters is proposed. This algorithm has both smoothing and tracking properties. Based on the developed wavelet-neurons the architecture of the wavelet-neuro-compressor and its learning algorithm are proposed. This compressor has the variety of advantages in comparison with conventional multilayer autoassociative perceptron "Bottle Neck" and, first of all, ability of information processing in form of the data stream.

W-neuron with multidimensional wavelet activation functions that has more wide ability in comparison to wavelet neuron is proposed. In this W-neuron the synaptic weights and centers, receptive field's parameters and shape of activation function are tuned both based on conventional square error criterion and robust learning one.

Based on proposed nodes the architectures of hybrid adaptive systems in terms of Takagi-Sugeno-Kang and ANFIS are synthesized. Such multilayer WNFSs have improved approximation properties and learning speed in comparison with their prototypes.

For the choice of system's architecture, we propose to tune it using evolving connectionist approach. Together with conventional approach, we propose to use Group Method of Data Handling too. This approach is close to the ideas of the deep learning and the cascade neural networks theory, allowed to form the architecture of WNFS in on-line mode.

The computational experiments results based on benchmarks and real data sets confirm the efficiency of developing approach.

Keywords: dynamic data mining, soft computing, wavelet neuro-fuzzy systems, hybrid GMDH neural network, prediction, identification

INTRODUCTION

Methods of scientific direction that is developed within computer science and is known as computational intelligence have been widely used to solve various problems of dynamic data mining [1, 2] recently. The very first reason behind advantages of the computational intelligence is the fact that they perform data processing in biologically plausible way, leading to necessary flexibility, adaptivity, linguistic interpretability of the designed models. Whereas computational intelligence theory and practice had been evolved initially in three relatively independent directions, namely, artificial neural networks, fuzzy systems, and evolutionary computations, nowadays both brand new directions of computational intelligence (rough sets, wavelet systems, liquid, granular, quantum, spiking computations) and combinations of known ones (neuro-fuzzy systems, wavelet-neuro-fuzzy systems, spiking neural networks, neo-fuzzy systems, reservoir neural networks) continue appearing.

Hybrid systems are the most effective systems of computational intelligence now, especially neuro-fuzzy and wavelet-neuro-fuzzy systems that combine neural networks' universal approximation ability, fuzzy inference systems' interpretability, compact representation of signal local properties based on wavelet transform, and still their architecture, as a rule, is fixed and redundant. In addition, number of neurons in each layer of the network is chosen on empirical grounds usually. Such unhandiness of the mentioned systems architecture requires unnecessary nodes and surplus parameters adjustment, thus affecting data processing performance. An alternative here is to adjust not only individual neurons but overall architecture also. In this way effective and compact systems can be produced regarding specific problem. That is the essential of one of the computational intelligence directions, evolving connectionist systems [2, 3], that is advancing steadily. It is pertinent to note that the concept of searching for optimal architecture of neural and neuro-fuzzy networks is close to the idea of the Group Method of Data Handling (GMDH), introduced by O. Ivakhnenko [4-6] in the middle of last century. The GMDH has demonstrated its efficiency in different areas of science and engineering, including neural networks optimal architecture design [7-11].

In this research, concepts of hybrid systems of computational intelligence, evolving connectionist systems, and GMDH have been combined to solve some data mining problems that require on-line solutions in sequence mode.

HYBRID NODES OF GMDH-WAVELET-NEURO-FUZZY SYSTEMS

Neo-Fuzzy Neuron and Wavelet Neuron

Let us consider a neo-fuzzy neuron whose architecture is shown in Figure 1.

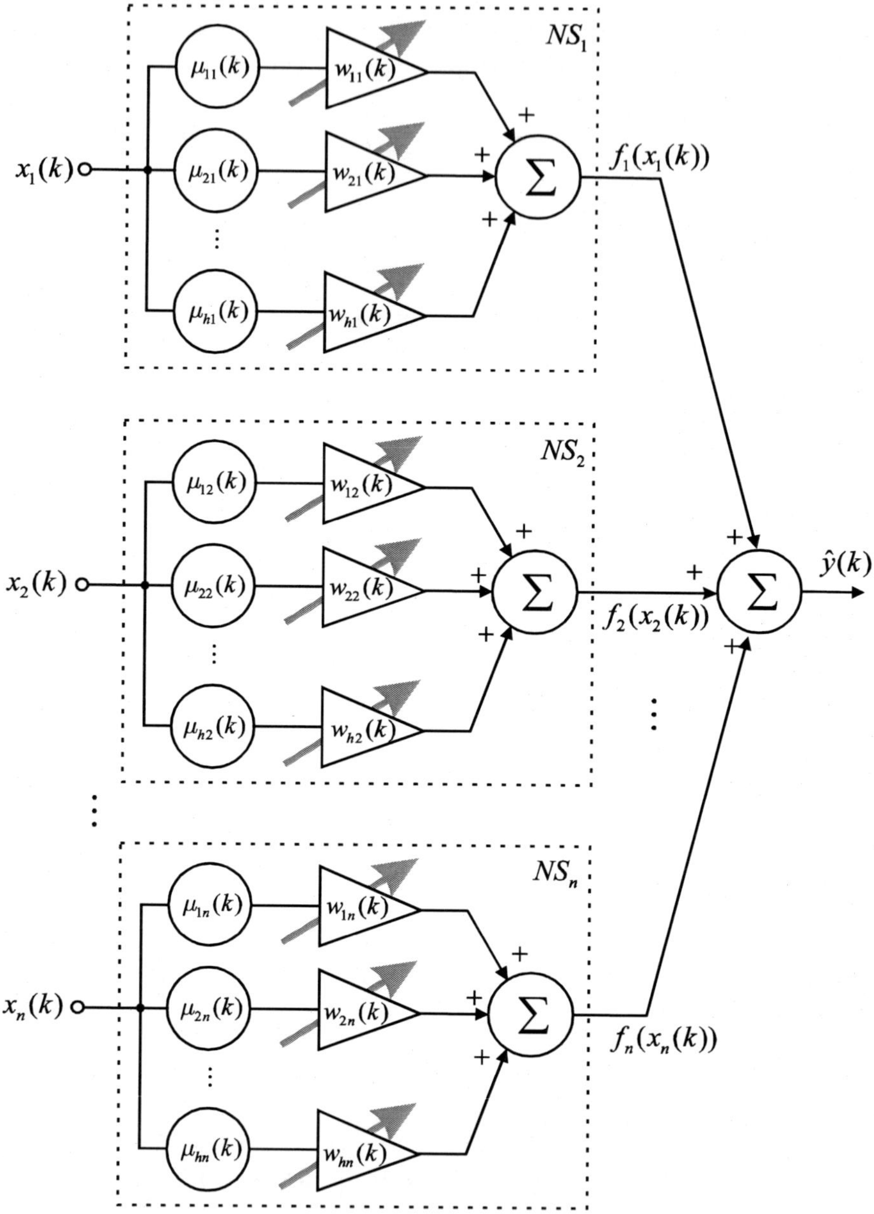

Figure 1. Neo-fuzzy neuron.

It has multi-input architecture with one output. The following advantages of neo-fuzzy neuron were intimated previously [12, 13]: high learning speed, computational simplicity, ability to find a global minimum of the learning criterion, and the fact its functioning is described by the set of fuzzy linguistic 'if-then' rules.

Neo-fuzzy neuron performs the following mapping:

$$\hat{y}(k)=\sum_{i=1}^{n} f_i(x_i(k)) \tag{1}$$

where $x_i(k)$ is the i -th input $(i=1,\ldots,n)$; $\hat{y}(k)$ is the system output; f is a nonlinear function; k is discrete time.

The structural units of neo-fuzzy neuron are nonlinear synapses NS_i that transform the i -th input signal as follows:

$$f_i(x_i(k))=\sum_{j=1}^{h} \mu_{ji}(x_i(k))w_{ji}(k-1) \tag{2}$$

where μ_{ji} is the membership function of neuro-fuzzy neuron; $w_{ji}(k-1)$ is the j -th adjustable synaptic weight of the i -th nonlinear synapse at the previous step $(k-1)$; h is the number of membership functions in the nonlinear synapse.

As is easy to see, in general, each nonlinear synapse can be described by h fuzzy rules

$$IF \quad x_i \quad IS \quad A_{ji} \; THEN \quad f_i=w_{ji}, \quad j=1,\ldots,h \tag{3}$$

where A_{ji} is the fuzzy set defined by membership function μ_{ji}; w_{ji} is a singleton (synaptic weight) in the consequent.

One can readily see that a nonlinear synapse in fact performs the fuzzy inference that is similar to 0-order Takagi-Sugeno system. As a rule, membership functions $\mu_{ji}(x_i)$ in antecedent have the conjugate-triangular shape shown in Figure 2 when value of signal x_i is within range $[x_{i,\min}, x_{i,\max}]$.

The membership functions can be written for preliminarily transformed input variables x_i (usually normalization $x_{i,\min} \le x_i \le x_{i,\max}$ is applied) as follows:

$$\mu_{ji}(x_i) = \begin{cases} \dfrac{x_i - c_{j-1,i}}{c_{i,j} - c_{j-1,i}}, & x_i \in [c_{j-1,i}, c_{j,i}], \\ \dfrac{c_{j+1,i} - x_i}{c_{j+1,i} - c_{j,i}}, & x_i \in [c_{j,i}, c_{j+1,i}], \mathbb{S} \\ 0, & x_i \notin [c_{j-1,i}, c_{j+1,i}] \end{cases} \tag{4}$$

where c_{ji} is the center of the j-th membership function of the i-the input that is chosen arbitrarily, but that is uniformly distributed over interval $[-1,1]$ that simplifies fuzzy inference process as input signal x_i fires those two adjacent membership functions only whose values sum equals unity (Ruspini partitioning), i.e.,

$$\sum_{j=1}^{h} \mu_{ji}(x_i(k)) = 1. \tag{5}$$

Example of such functions is shown in Figure 2.

Results of fuzzy inference obtained from defuzzification following the center of gravity technique can be presented in a simple form:

$$f_i(x_i) = w_{ji}\mu_{ji}(x_i) + w_{j+1,i}\mu_{j+1,i}(x_i), \tag{6}$$

and value of output $\hat{y}$ is calculated according to expression (1).

Usually the learning criterion is a quadratic error function

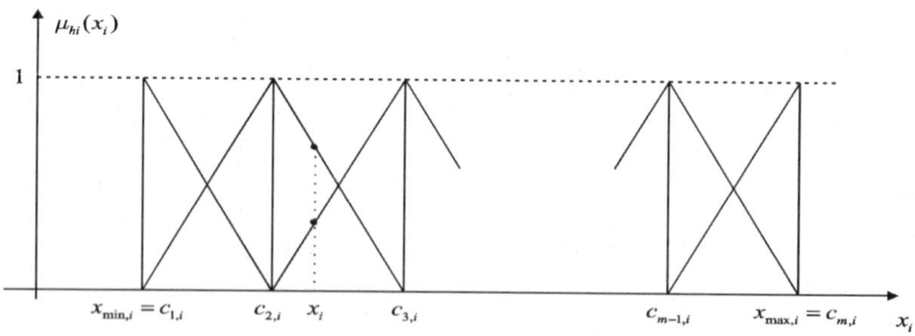

Figure 2. Membership functions satisfying Ruspini partitioning.

$$E(k)=\frac{1}{2}(y(k)-\hat{y}(k))^2=\frac{1}{2}e^2(k)=\frac{1}{2}\left(y(k)-\sum_{i=1}^{n}\sum_{j=1}^{h}w_{ji}(k-1)\mu_{ji}(x_i(k))\right)^2 \quad (7)$$

that is minimized via the gradient method taking here the following form:

$$w_{ji}(k+1)=w_{ji}(k)+\eta e(k+1)\mu_{ji}(x_i(k+1)). \quad (8)$$

In order to increase the learning speed [14, 15], one can utilize one-step optimal algorithm of Kaczmarz-Widrow-Hoff [16, 17] as follows:

$$w(k+1)=w(k)+\frac{y(k+1)-w^T(k)\mu(x(k+1))}{\|\mu(x(k+1))\|^2}\mu(x(k+1)) \quad (9)$$

where $\mu(x(k+1))=(\mu_{11}(x_1(k+1)),\ldots,\mu_{1h}(x_1(k+1)),\ldots,\mu_{2h}(x_2(k+1)),\ldots,\mu_{nh}(x_n(k+1)))^T$ – $nh\times 1$ is a membership functions vector; $w(k)=(w_{11}(k),\ldots,w_{1h}(k),\ldots,w_{2h}(k),\ldots,w_{nh}(k))^T$ – $nh\times 1$ is a vector of synaptic weights.

An exponentially weighted modification of method (9) is used on a number of occasions:

$$\begin{cases} w(k+1)=w(k)+r^{-1}(k+1)e_I(k+1)\mu(k+1), \\ r(k+1)=\beta r(k)+\|\mu(k+1)\|^2, \quad 0\le\beta\le 1 \end{cases} \quad (10)$$

(here $e_I(k)=y(k)-\hat{y}(k)$) that has both filtering and tracking properties.

If the training set is defined a priori, learning may be performed in batch mode in one epoch via conventional least squares method.

Since triangular membership functions do not provide approximation quality of non-stationary process model in some cases, it makes sense to design adaptive wavelet function of activation-membership that would gain advantage of wavelet function to determine local specific.

Let us consider architecture of wavelet neuron [18] that is shown in Figure 3.

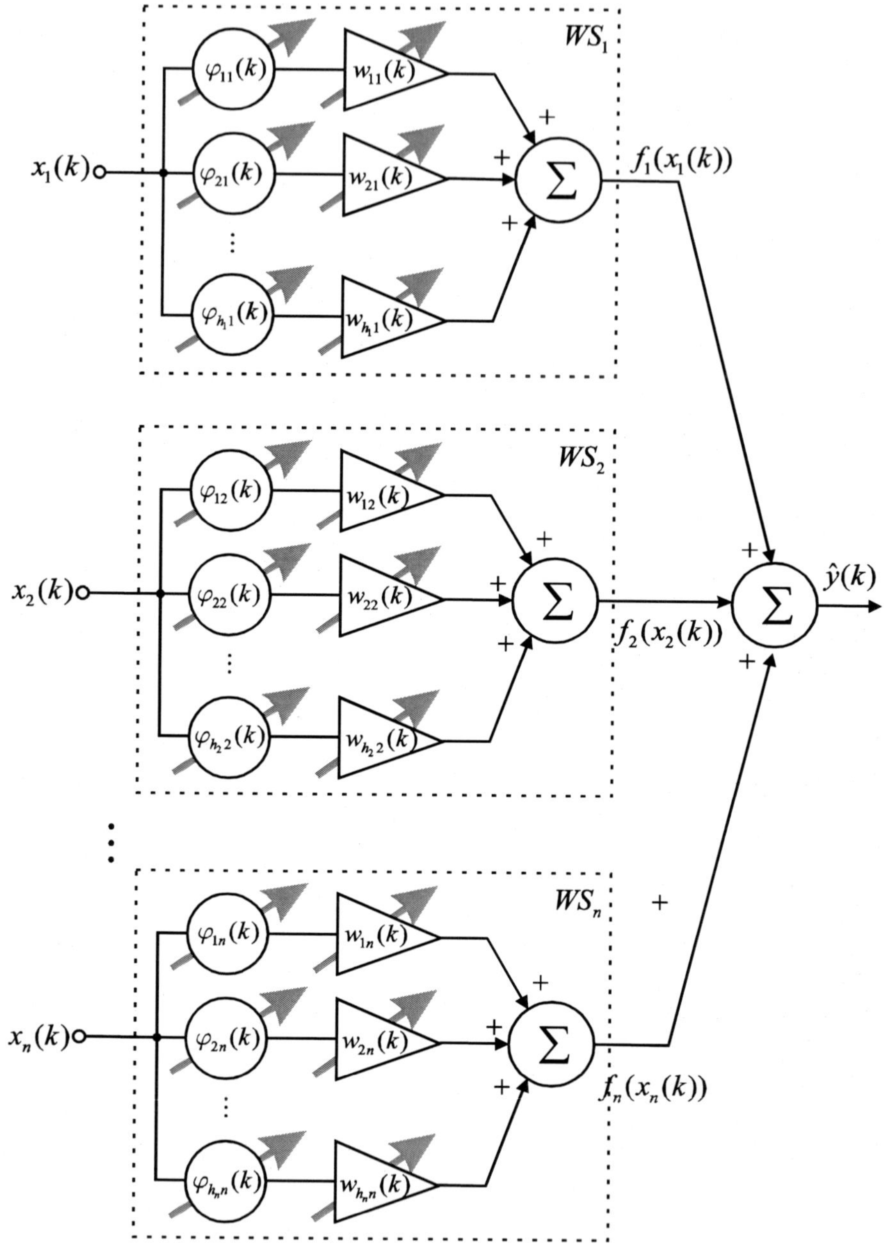

Figure 3. Wavelet neuron.

As it can be seen, the wavelet neuron is similar to neo-fuzzy neuron architecture, but, instead of conventional adjustable synaptic weights, it contains wavelet synapses WS_i, $i=1,2,\ldots,n$ whose adjustable parameters are not weights only $w_{ji}(k)$, but also parameters of center, width, and shape of adaptive wavelet activation-membership function $\varphi_{ji}(x_i(k))$.

When input of wavelet neuron gets vector signal

$$x(k)=(x_1(k),x_2(k),\ldots,x_n(k))^T,$$

its output produces a scalar

$$\hat{y}(k)=\sum_{i=1}^{n} f_i(x(k))=\sum_{i=1}^{n}\sum_{j=1}^{h_i} w_{ji}(k-1)\varphi_{ji}(x_i(k)) \qquad (11)$$

that is defined both by adjustable weights $w_{ji}(k)$, and by the wavelet functions being used.

One can use any families of analytical wavelets [19] as activation-membership functions in wavelet neuron, e.g., Polywog wavelets, Rasp wavelets, Morlet wavelet and others.

Here, we will use one-dimensional adaptive wavelet-function of activation-membership proposed in [20, 21]:

$$\varphi_{ji}(x_i(k))=(1-\alpha_{ji}(k)t_{ji}^2(k))\exp\left(-\frac{t_{ji}^2(k)}{2}\right) \qquad (12)$$

where $t_{ji}(k)=\ x_i(k)-c_{ji}(k)\ \sigma_{ji}^{-1}(k)$; $c_{ji}(k)$ is the parameter that defines location of the function center; $\sigma_{ji}(k)$ is the parameter that defines the function width; $\alpha_{ji}(k)$ is the parameter that defines shape of the wavelet function.

Adjustable parameter α_{ji} allows of adjusting shape of adaptive wavelet function of activation-membership during learning. If $\alpha_{ji}=0$, then a Gaussian function is produced, if $\alpha_{ji}=1$, then Mexican Hat wavelet function is produced, and if $0<\alpha_{ji}<1$, then a hybrid activation-membership function is produced.

Various adaptive wavelet functions of activation-membership driven by the mentioned parameters are shows on Figure 4.

An additional point to emphasize here is that wavelet function oscillativity does not contradict to membership function unipolarity since negative values can be treated as low membership levels or non-membership [22, 23].

Learning task is to choose synaptic weights $w_{ji}(k)$, centers $c_{ji}(k)$, widths $\sigma_{ji}^{-1}(k)$, and shape parameters $\alpha_{ji}(k)$ of wavelet function of activation-membership on each iteration k that will optimize the considered quality criterion.

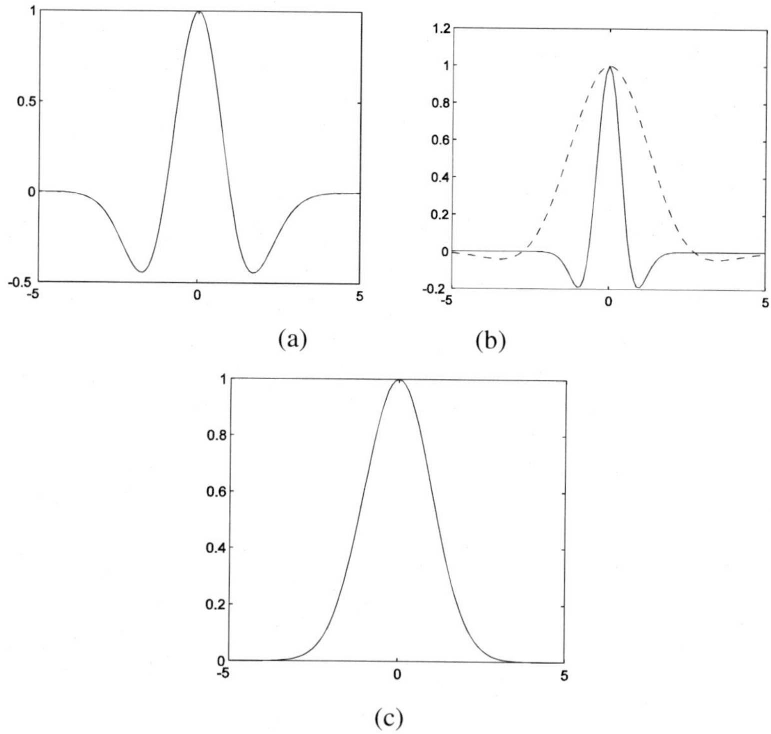

Figure 4. Adaptive wavelet functions of activation-membership: a – $\alpha = 1, \sigma = 1$; b – dashed line $\alpha = 0.3, \sigma = 1.5$, solid line $\alpha = 0.6, \sigma = 0.5$; c – $\alpha = 0, \sigma = 1$.

As a learning criterion of wavelet neuron, a quadratic error function is used that is expressed in wavelet neuron notation as follows:

$$E(k)=\frac{1}{2}(y(k)-\hat{y}(k))^2=\frac{1}{2}e^2(k)=\frac{1}{2}(y(k)-\sum_{i=1}^{n}\sum_{j=1}^{h_i}w_{ji}(k-1)\varphi_{ji}(x_i(k)))^2 \quad (13)$$

(here $y(k)$ is the external learning signal), and its derivatives subject to adjustable parameters have the form

$$\frac{\partial E(k)}{\partial w_{ji}(k)}=-e(k)\varphi_{ji}(x_i(k))=-e(k)(1-\alpha_{ij}(k)t_{ji}^2(k))\exp\left(-\frac{t_{ji}^2(k)}{2}\right)=-e(k)J_{ji}^{w}(k), \quad (14)$$

$$\frac{\partial E(k)}{\partial c_{ji}(k)}=-e(k)w_{ji}(k)\sigma_{ji}^{-1}(k)((2\alpha_{ji}(k)+1)t_{ji}(k)-\alpha_{ji}(k)t_{ji}^3(k))\exp\left(-\frac{t_{ji}^2(k)}{2}\right)= \quad (15)$$
$$=-e(k)J_{ji}^{c}(k),$$

$$\frac{\partial E(k)}{\partial \sigma_{ji}^{-1}(k)}=-e(k)w_{ji}(k)(x_i(k)-c_{ji}(k))((2\alpha_{ji}(k)+1)t_{ji}(k)-\alpha_{ji}(k)t_{ji}^3(k))\times$$
$$\times\exp\left(-\frac{t_{ji}^2(k)}{2}\right)=-e(k)J_{ji}^{\sigma}(k), \quad (16)$$

$$\frac{\partial E(k)}{\partial \alpha_{ji}(k)}=e(k)w_{ji}(k)t_{ji}^2(k)\exp\left(-\frac{t_{ji}^2(k)}{2}\right)=-e(k)J_{ji}^{\alpha}(k). \quad (17)$$

Then, by applying gradient procedure to minimize (13), we can express learning method of wavelet neuron as follows:

$$\begin{cases} w_{ji}(k+1)=w_{ji}(k)+\eta^{w}(k+1)e(k+1)J_{ji}^{w}(k+1), \\ c_{ji}(k+1)=c_{ji}(k)+\eta^{c}(k+1)e(k+1)J_{ji}^{c}(k+1), \\ \sigma_{ji}^{-1}(k+1)=\sigma_{ji}^{-1}(k)+\eta^{\sigma}(k+1)e(k+1)J_{ji}^{\sigma}(k+1), \\ \alpha_{ji}(k+1)=\alpha_{ji}(k)+\eta^{\alpha}(k+1)e(k+1)J_{ji}^{\alpha}(k+1) \end{cases} \quad (18)$$

where scalars $\eta^{w}(k)$, $\eta^{c}(k)$, $\eta^{\sigma}(k)$, $\eta^{\alpha}(k)$ define learning step in adjustable parameters space.

By introducing $(h_i \times 1)$ – vectors of variables $\varphi_i(x_i(k)) = (\varphi_{1i}(x_i(k)), \ldots, \varphi_{h_i i}(x_i(k)))^T$, $w_i(k) = (w_{1i}(k), \ldots, w_{h_i i}(k))^T$, $c_i(k) = (c_{1i}(k), \ldots, c_{h_i i}(k))^T$, $\sigma_i^{-1}(k) = (\sigma_{1i}^{-1}(k), \ldots, \sigma_{h_i i}^{-1}(k))^T$, $\alpha_i(k) = (\alpha_{1i}(k), \ldots, \alpha_{h_i i}(k))^T$, $t_i(k) = (t_{1i}(k), \ldots, t_{h_i i}(k))^T$, $J_i^w(k) = (J_{1i}^w(k), \ldots, J_{h_i i}^w(k))^T$, $J_i^c(k) = (J_{1i}^c(k), \ldots, J_{h_i i}^c(k))^T$, $J_i^\sigma(k) = (J_{1i}^\sigma(k), \ldots, J_{h_i i}^\sigma(k))^T$, $J_i^\alpha(k) = (J_{1i}^\alpha(k), \ldots, J_{h_i i}^\alpha(k))^T$, we can state gradient procedure of the i -th wavelet synapse learning method:

$$\begin{cases} w_i(k+1) = w_i(k) + \eta^w(k+1)e(k+1)J_i^w(k+1), \\ c_i(k+1) = c_i(k) + \eta^c(k+1)e(k+1)J_i^c(k+1), \\ \sigma_i^{-1}(k+1) = \sigma_i^{-1}(k) + \eta^\sigma(k+1)e(k+1)J_i^\sigma(k+1), \\ \alpha_i(k+1) = \alpha_i(k) + \eta^\alpha(k+1)e(k+1)J_i^\alpha(k+1). \end{cases} \tag{19}$$

It is possible to improve convergence of the learning processes by switching from gradient procedures to the Levenberg-Marquardt algorithm for adjusting of neural networks [24].

Using inverse of sum of matrices lemma and performing obvious transformation [25], we can write learning algorithms for real time case:

$$\begin{cases} w_i(k+1) = w_i(k) + \dfrac{e(k+1)J_i^w(k+1)}{r_i^w(k+1)}, \quad r_i^w(k+1) = \beta r_i^w(k) + \| J_i^w(k+1) \|^2, \\ c_i(k+1) = c_i(k) + \dfrac{e(k+1)J_i^c(k+1)}{r_i^c(k+1)}, \quad r_i^c(k+1) = \beta r_i^c(k) + \| J_i^c(k+1) \|^2, \\ \sigma_i^{-1}(k+1) = \sigma_i^{-1}(k) + \dfrac{e(k+1)J_i^\sigma(k+1)}{r_i^\sigma(k+1)}, \quad r_i^\sigma(k+1) = \beta r_i^\sigma(k) + \| J_i^\sigma(k+1) \|^2, \\ \alpha_i(k+1) = \alpha_i(k) + \dfrac{e(k+1)J_i^\alpha(k+1)}{r_i^\alpha(k+1)}, \quad r_i^\alpha(k+1) = \beta r_i^\alpha(k) + \| J_i^\alpha(k+1) \|^2, 0 \le \beta \le 1 \end{cases} \tag{20}$$

where β is the forgetting parameter.

It is clear that given $\beta = 1$, method (21), (22) acquires stochastic approximation qualities of adaptive Goodwin-Ramadge-Caines algorithm [26], and given $\beta = 0$, it becomes Widrow-Hoff algorithm that is widely used in artificial neural networks theory.

Thus, modified learning methods usage does not complicate numerical implementation of wavelet synapses adjusting procedures virtually and increases speed of their convergence.

On the base of wavelet-neuron architecture, let us introduce two-layered wavelet neural architecture shown in Figure 5 that allows of solving multidimensional time series compression problem.

When time series $X = \{x^1(k), x^2(k), \ldots, x^n(k)\}$ is fed to wavelet-neuro-compressor input, it outputs signal

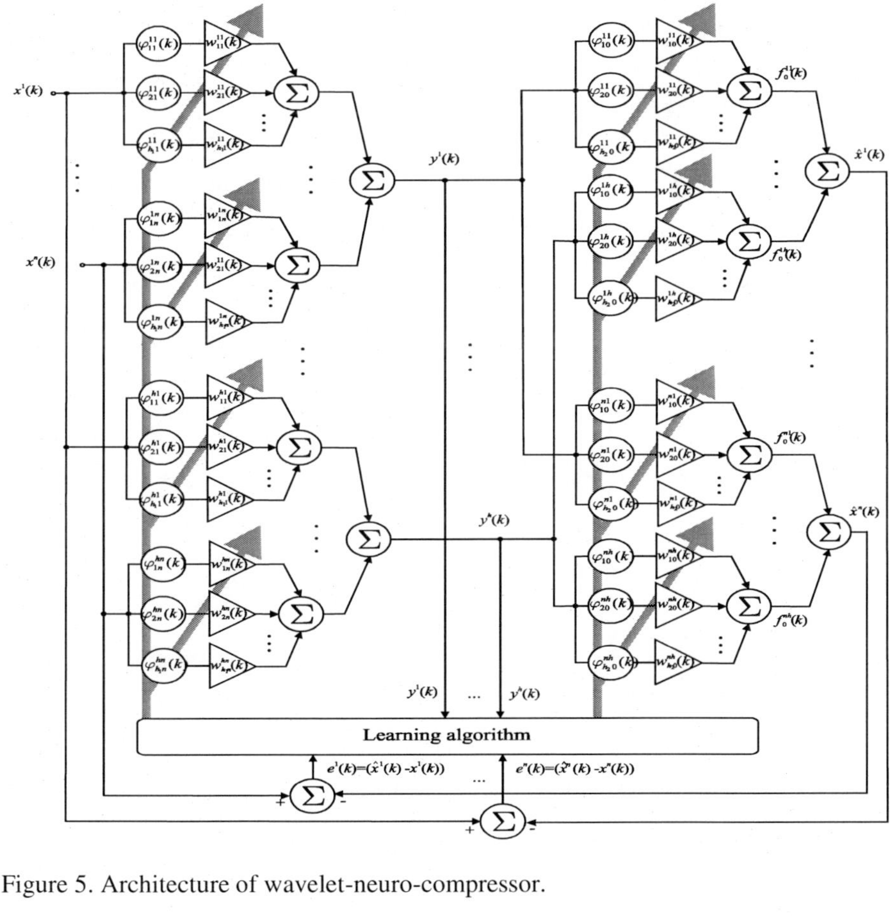

Figure 5. Architecture of wavelet-neuro-compressor.

$$\hat{x}^i(k)=\sum_{m=1}^{h}\sum_{j=1}^{h_2}\varphi_{j0}^{im}(y^m(k))w_{j0}^{im}(k-1)=$$
$$=\sum_{m=1}^{h}\sum_{j=1}^{h_2}\varphi_{j0}^{im}\left(\sum_{i=1}^{n}\sum_{l=1}^{h_1}\varphi_{li}^{mi}(x^i(k))w_{li}^{mi}(k-1)\right)w_{j0}^{im}(k-1) \quad (21)$$

where $\varphi_{li}^{mi}(\bullet)$, $\varphi_{j0}^{im}(\bullet)$ are wavelet activation functions of the first and second layer correspondingly, $w_{li}^{mi}(k-1)$, $w_{j0}^{im}(k-1)$ are synaptic weights of input and output layer correspondingly, $y^m(k)$ is the m-th component of compressed multidimensional time series.

In each wavelet synapse, wavelets are implemented so that they differ from one another by center and width parameters that are adjusted along with synaptic weights by a particular learning method.

Wavelet-neuro-compressor architecture consists of two layers: hidden one that has hn wavelet synapses with h_1 wavelet functions in each, and output one that has hn wavelet synapses with h_2 wavelet functions.

In order to perform adaptive adjusting of wavelet-neuro-compressor, we will use an adaptive wavelet function of activation-membership whose parameters and shape would be adjusted during learning of the compression system. It has the following form for the hidden layer:

$$\varphi_{li}^{mi}(x^i(x(k)))=\ 1-\alpha_{li}^{mi}(k)(\tau_{li}^{mi}(x^i(k)))^2\ \exp\left(-\frac{(\tau_{li}^{mi}(x^i(k)))^2}{2}\right) \quad (22)$$

and for the second layer

$$\varphi_{j0}^{im}(y^m(x(k)))=\ 1-\alpha_{j0}^{im}(k)(\tau_{j0}^{im}(x^i(k)))^2\ \exp\left(-\frac{(\tau_{j0}^{im}(x^i(k)))^2}{2}\right) \quad (23)$$

where $\tau_{li}^{mi}(x^i(k))=(x^i(k)-c_{li}^{mi}(k))(\sigma_{li}^{mi}(k))^{-1}$, $\tau_{j0}^{im}(x^i(k))=(x^i(k)-c_{j0}^{im}(k))(\sigma_{j0}^{im}(k))^{-1}$, $\alpha_{li}^{mi}(k)$, $\alpha_{j0}^{im}(k)$ is an adjustable parameter $(0\le\alpha\le 1)$.

Using the conventional learning criterion

$$E^i(k)=\frac{1}{2}\left(x^i(k)-\sum_{i=1}^{n}f_0^{im}(y^m(k))\right)^2, \tag{24}$$

we can write learning method for synaptic weights and all wavelet activation-membership functions' parameters of the first layer as follows:

$$\begin{cases} w_{li}^{mi}(k+1)=w_{li}^{mi}(k)+\eta^w e^i(k+1)[f_0^{im}(y^m(k+1))]'\varphi_{li}^{mi}(x^i(k+1)), \\ c_{li}^{mi}(k+1)=c_{li}^{mi}(k)+\eta^c e^i(k+1)[f_0^{im}(y^m(k+1))]'w_{li}^{mi}(k+1)\dfrac{\partial\varphi_{li}^{mi}(x^i(k+1))}{\partial c_{li}^{mi}}, \\ (\sigma_{li}^{mi})^{-1}(k+1)=(\sigma_{li}^{mi})^{-1}(k)+\eta^\sigma e^i(k+1)[f_0^{im}(y^m(k+1))]'w_{li}^{mi}(k+1)\dfrac{\partial\varphi_{li}^{mi}(x^i(k+1))}{\partial(\sigma_{li}^{mi})^{-1}}, \\ \alpha_{li}^{mi}(k+1)=\alpha_{li}^{mi}(k)+\eta^\alpha e^i(k+1)[f_0^{im}(y^m(k+1))]'w_{li}^{mi}(k+1)\dfrac{\partial\varphi_{li}^{mi}(x^i(k+1))}{\partial\alpha_{li}^{mi}} \end{cases} \tag{25}$$

where $[f_0^{im}(y^m(k))]'=\sum_{j=1}^{h_2}w_{j0}^{im}\dfrac{\partial\varphi_{j0}^{im}(y^m(k))}{\partial y^m(k)}$.

Learning method of the second layer is based on the criterion

$$E^i(k)=\frac{1}{2}(x^i(k)-\hat{x}^i(k))^2=\frac{1}{2}e^{i2}(k). \tag{26}$$

Thus, learning method of synaptic weights and all parameters of wavelet activation-membership functions of the second layer has the form

$$\begin{cases} w_{j0}^{im}(k+1)=w_{j0}^{im}(k)+\eta_0 e^i(k+1)\varphi_{j0}^{im}(y^m(k+1)), \\ c_{j0}^{im}(k+1)=c_{j0}^{im}(k)+\eta_0^c e^i(k+1)w_{j0}^{im}(k+1)\dfrac{\partial\varphi_{j0}^{im}(y^m(k+1))}{\partial c_{j0}^{im}}, \\ (\sigma_{j0}^{im})^{-1}(k+1)=(\sigma_{j0}^{im})^{-1}(k)+\eta_0^\sigma e^i(k+1)w_{j0}^{im}(k+1)\dfrac{\partial\varphi_{j0}^{im}(y^m(k+1))}{\partial(\sigma_{j0}^{im})^{-1}}, \\ \alpha_{j0}^{im}(k+1)=\alpha_{j0}^{im}(k)+\eta_0^\alpha e^i(k+1)w_{j0}^{im}(k+1)\dfrac{\partial\varphi_{j0}^{im}(y^m(k+1))}{\partial\alpha_{j0}^{im}}. \end{cases} \tag{27}$$

Just summarizing, we can state that wavelet-neuro-compressor allows of compressing and detecting both local properties of data presented as 'object-feature' tables and non-stationary nonlinear time series that is an advantage as compared to existing methods.

Adaptive W-Neuron with Multidimensional Wavelet Activation-Membership Functions

The most known and popular now are multilayered feed forward networks of three-layered perceptron type whose nodes are so-called P-neurons with monotonous activation functions. Such popularity arose from their universal approximation ability along with relatively compact representation of the nonlinear system being modeled.

The major shortcoming of multilayered networks is the low learning speed caused by error back propagation that complicates their usage in on-line mode.

An alternative to multilayered artificial neural networks are radial basis functions neural networks that have one hidden layer consisting of so-called R-neurons, and learning of such networks is performed in the output layer only, that is adaptive linear associator [27, 28].

The major advantage of radial basis function neural networks is high learning speed in the output layer that is explained by linearity in adjustable parameters in the network model. Yet, the question of R-neurons distribution remains open, failure to solve it leads to the curse of dimensionality. Though usage of clustering methods allows of reducing the network size, but it precludes from network operating in sequential mode. It is notable that [29] presents gradient recurrent procedure of center c_j parameters component-wise adjustment but its convergence is significantly slow.

In this section we consider structure of adaptive W-neuron with multidimensional wavelet activation-membership functions and its learning methods utilizing both quadratic and robust criteria that have higher convergence speed and improved approximation ability and that allow of processing non-stationary signals with abnormal outliers. Architecture of W-neuron can be used as a stand-alone network or as a building unit of evolving networks, in particular as a neuron of hybrid GMDH-neural network [30, 31].

There are a lot of one-dimensional activation functions that sometimes do not allow of achieving required accuracy of forecasting, identification, and emulation of non-stationary nonlinear time series since they are not able of local properties detecting.

As it was noted before, the frequently used neural networks with multidimensional activation functions are radial basis function neural networks that carry out T. Cover's idea that linearly inseparable task of pattern recognition in space $\mathbf{R}^n$ may become linear separable in the space of higher dimensionality $\mathbf{R}^h$. Properties of such networks are fully defined by radial basis functions φ that are used in neurons of hidden layer and form a certain basis for vectors-patterns x. Radial basis function in general form

$$\varphi(x) = \varphi(\| x - c \|, \sigma) = \varphi(s, \sigma)$$

is a multidimensional function that depends on distance $s = \| x - c \|$ between input vector x and own center c and width parameter σ that defines local area of input space that activated the given function. Thus each neuron of hidden layer calculates distance between input vector and its own center and performs a certain nonlinear transformation $\varphi(s, \sigma)$ of them.

It is significant that, in contrast to monotonous activation functions of multilayered networks, radial basis functions, as a rule, are symmetric and cover a relatively narrow area of input space. Fairly often radial basis functions are bell-shaped and can be expressed as derivatives of conventional neurons activation functions.

In the most cases of practical applications, nodes centers c_i and width parameters σ_i are hard-set, and synaptic weights w_i are adjusted only. In solving more complex tasks (such as classification, forecasting, pattern recognition), it is reasonable to adjust all parameters of activation functions.

In neural networks of radial basis function type, besides the most popular Gaussian whose plot is shown in Figure 6 and that has form

$$\varphi_1(\| x - c \|, \sigma) = \varphi_1(s, \sigma) = \exp\left(-\frac{s^2}{2\sigma^2} \right), \tag{28}$$

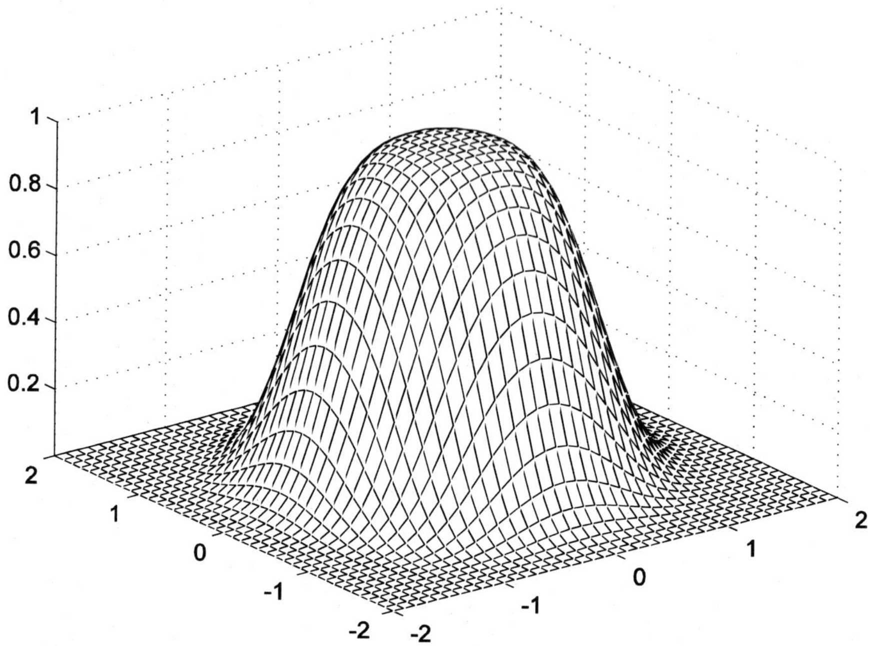

Figure 6. Multidimensional Gaussian activation function.

the following kernel functions are used as well:

- multiquadratic:

$$\varphi_2(s,\sigma) = (s^2 + \sigma^2)^{\frac{1}{2}}, \tag{29}$$

- inverse multiquadratic:

$$\varphi_3(s,\sigma) = (s^2 + \sigma^2)^{-\frac{1}{2}}, \tag{30}$$

- spline:

$$\varphi_4(s,\sigma) = \left(\frac{s}{\sigma}\right)^2 log\left(\frac{s}{\sigma}\right), \tag{31}$$

and others

$$\Phi_5(s,\sigma)=\left(1+\frac{s}{\sigma}\right)^{-2}, \qquad (32)$$

$$\Phi_6(s,\sigma)=cos\left(\frac{s}{\sigma}\right), \qquad (33)$$

$$\Phi_7(s,\sigma)=1-\left|\frac{s}{\sigma}\right| \qquad (34)$$

and though not all of them are bell-shaped (29), (31) (32), their usage in tasks of identification, modelling, and forecasting appeared to be expedient.

As mentioned before, activation function (28) whose features can be extended using multidimensional Gaussian of the following general form receives widespread use:

$$\varphi(x)=\varphi(\|x-c\|,\Sigma)=\exp(-(x-c)^T\Sigma^{-1}(x-c))=\exp(-\|x-c\|^2_{\Sigma^{-1}}) \qquad (35)$$

where covariance matrix Σ defines shape, size, and orientation of radial basis function receptive field.

Given $\Sigma=\sigma^2\mathbf{I}$ (here, $\mathbf{I}$ – $(n\times n)$-identity matrix), receptive field is a hypersphere with center c and radius σ; given $\Sigma=diag(\sigma_1^2,\sigma_2^2,\ldots,\sigma_n^2)$ it is hyperellipsoid whose axes coincides with axes of input space and have length $2\sigma_i$ via i-th axis, and, finally, given Σ is a non-diagonal positive definite matrix

$$\Sigma=S^T\Lambda S, \qquad (36)$$

matrix of eigenvalues Λ defines shape and size of receptive field, and matrix of orthogonal rotation S defines its orientation.

On the other hand, various even wavelet function are used as activation functions in wavelet neural networks, the most popular among them is the Mexican Hat wavelet. As is easy to see, activation function for a network node is chosen on empirical grounds.

Using one-dimensional wavelet activation-membership function as a basis, let us introduce mathematical model of multidimensional adaptive wavelet function of activation-membership that uses matrix $Q_j(k)$ instead of width parameter $\sigma_j(k)$, i.e., the used metric is not Euclidean, but Mahalanobis one or, in more general form, Itakura-Saito metric [32] that has the form [20]

$$\varphi_j(\tau_j(x(k))) = 1 - \alpha_j(k)\tau_j^2(x(k)) \exp\left(-\frac{\tau_j^2(x(k))}{2}\right) \quad (37)$$

where $\tau_j(x(k)) = ((x(k) - c_j(k))^T Q_j(k)^{-1}(x(k) - c_j(k)))$; $x(k) = (x_1(k), x_2(k), \ldots, x_n(k))^T$ is vector of inputs; $c_j(k) = (c_{j1}(k), c_{j2}(k), \ldots, c_{jn}(k))^T$ is vector of centers of wavelet activation-membership functions in n-dimensional space; $Q_j(k)$ is $(n \times n)$-matrix of receptive fields of wavelet activation-membership functions that defines orientation of function in n-dimensional space; $\alpha_j(k)$ is an adjustable parameter that defines shape of wavelet activation-membership function.

Thus, receptive neurons – hyperellipsoids of W-neuron can be of arbitrary orientation regarding axes coordinates of space X that extends adaptive compartmental W-neuron features.

Adjustable parameter $\alpha_j(k)$ allows of adjusting shape of activation function during learning of compartmental adaptive W-neuron, and $\alpha_j = 0$ yields Gaussian activation function, $\alpha_j = 1$ yields Mexican Hat wavelet function, and $0 < \alpha_j < 1$ yields hybrid wavelet activation-membership function.

Figure 7 shows possible shapes of adaptive wavelet activation-membership function given different matrices Q_j and parameter α_j when $n = 2$.

In order to initialize W-neuron, it is necessary to build a grid of adaptive wavelet activation-membership functions to covering input space. In the general case, such grid may be build in two ways: by uniform distribution of wavelet functions in space or via clustering procedures.

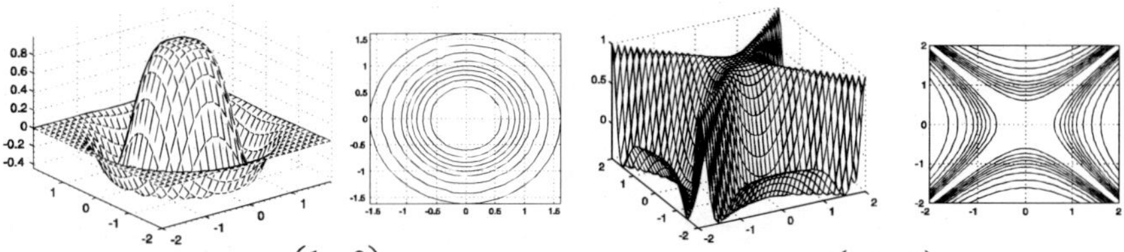

a) $Q^{-1} = \begin{pmatrix} 1 & 0 \\ 0 & 1 \end{pmatrix}, \alpha = 1$

b) $Q^{-1} = \begin{pmatrix} -1 & 0 \\ 0 & 1 \end{pmatrix}, \alpha = 1$

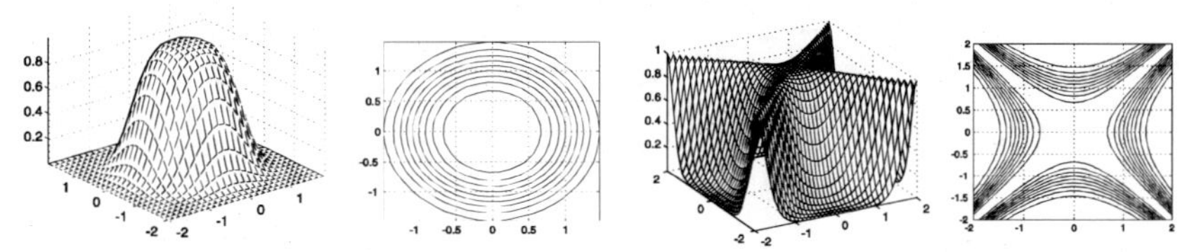

c) $Q^{-1} = \begin{pmatrix} 1 & 0 \\ 0 & 1 \end{pmatrix}, \alpha = 0$

d) $Q^{-1} = \begin{pmatrix} -1 & 0 \\ 0 & 1 \end{pmatrix}, \alpha = 0$

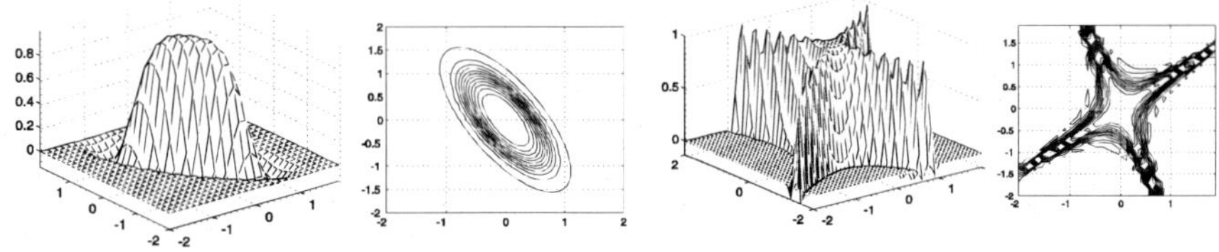

e) $Q^{-1} = \begin{pmatrix} 4 & 3 \\ 1 & 2 \end{pmatrix}, \alpha = 0.5$

f) $Q^{-1} = \begin{pmatrix} -4 & 3 \\ 1 & 2 \end{pmatrix}, \alpha = 0.5$

Figure 7. Multidimensional adaptive wavelet activation-membership functions.

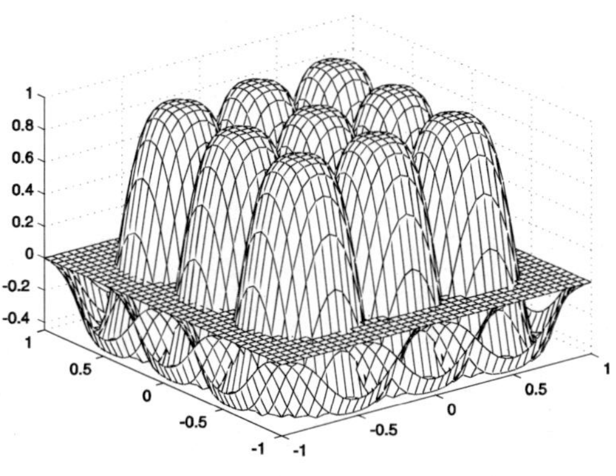

Figure 8. Grid based on multidimensional adaptive wavelet activation-membership functions in three-dimensional case.

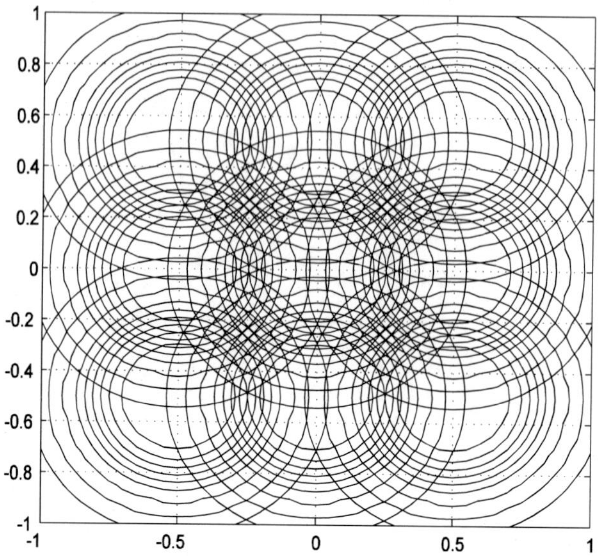

Figure 9. Grid based on multidimensional adaptive wavelet activation-membership functions in two-dimensional case.

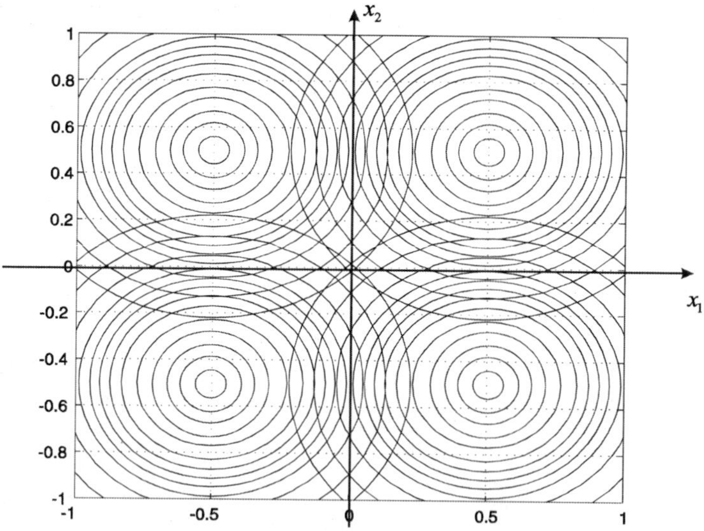

Figure 10. Grid based on lesser number of multidimensional adaptive wavelet activation-membership functions.

Thus, if input data are normalized beforehand in such way $-1 \leq x_i(k) \leq 1$, this adaptive wavelet activation-membershi functions in different forms is shown in Figure 8 in three-dimensional form and in Figure 9 in two-dimensional form.

As a rule, width parameter σ for Gaussian is chosen at level $\sigma \leq 0.33$ in order to cover input space fully. In case of adaptive wavelet activation-membership functions, as shown in Figure 9, if identical width parameters are chosen, the functions overlap significantly due to wave-like behavior of wavelet function. Thus, it is possible to use significantly less number of functions to build grid based on adaptive wavelet activation-membership functions as shown in Figure 10. In order to avoid 'holes' in space of activation functions, renormalization should take place during W-neuron learning.

Considering equivalence of RBF neural networks and fuzzy inference systems [33, 34] as well as possibility to use even wavelets as membership functions [22, 23], within unification paradigm [35], it is possible to introduce a hybrid system – compartmental W-neuron (wavelon) that can learn fast similar to RBF neural networks, has interpretability inherited from fuzzy inference systems, and has advantages in local properties of signals detection inherited from wavelet activation functions [36, 36].

Let us consider two-layered architecture shown in Figure 11 that is actually identical to conventional RBF neural network.

The zero layer of the architecture is receptive and at the current time k it receives input signal in vector form

$$x(k) = \left(x_1(k), x_2(k), \ldots, x_n(k) \right)^T. \tag{38}$$

In contrast to radial basis function neural networks, the hidden layer consists not of R-neurons, but of adaptive wavelet activation-membership of the form (37) whose parameters $(c_j(k), Q_j^{-1}(k), \alpha_j(k))$ are adjusted during learning.

And, finally, the output layer is a conventional adaptive linear associator with adjustable synaptic weights w_j

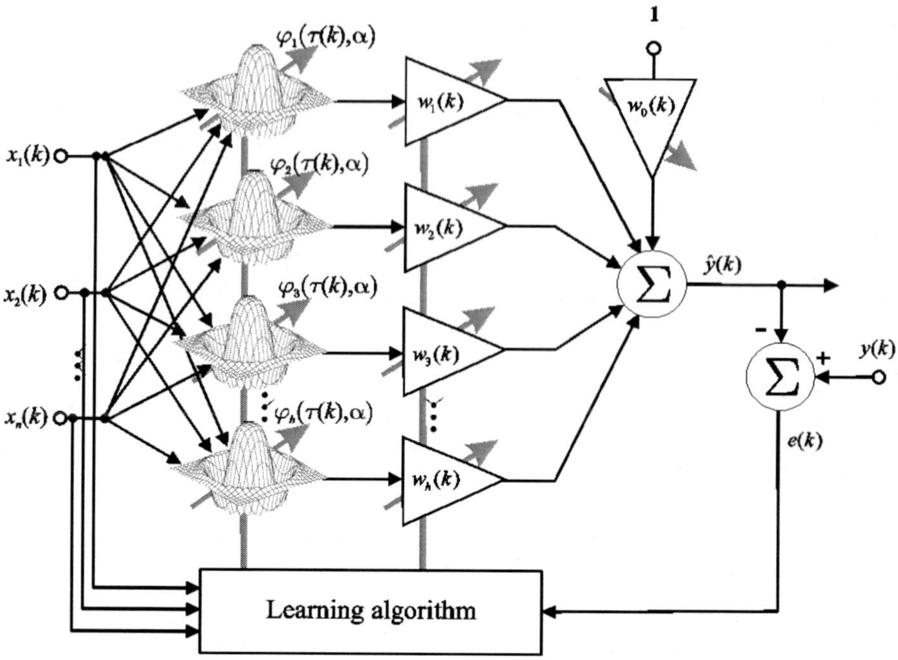

Figure 11. Architecture of W-neuron with multidimensional wavelet activation-membership functions.

$$\hat{y}(k) = w_0(k-1) + \sum_{j=1}^{h} w_j(k-1)\varphi_j(\tau_j(x(k))) = w(k-1)^T \varphi(\tau(x(k))) \quad (39)$$

where $\varphi_0(x(k)) \equiv 1$; $w(k) = (w_0(k), w_1(k), \ldots, w_h(k))^T$; $\varphi(\tau(k)) = (1, \varphi_1(\tau_1(x(k))),$ $\ldots, \varphi_h(\tau_h(x(k)))$.

Thus, we consider the parameters of W-neuron to be adjusted during learning will be $(h+1)$ synaptic weights w_j, h $(n \times 1)$–vectors c_j and h $(n \times n)$–matrices Q_j^{-1}. Such networks contains $h(1+n+n^2)+1$ adjusted parameters in total.

Since $(h+1) \times 1$ vector of synaptic weights w is linearly presented in the networks model, we can use any adaptive identification algorithm [38] to adjust it. First of all, it is either conventional least squares method of various forms, the simplest among them is its recurrent modification

$$\begin{cases} w(k+1) = w(k) + \dfrac{P(k)(y(k+1) - w^T(k)\varphi(\tau(x(k+1))))\varphi(\tau(x(k+1)))}{1+\varphi^T(\tau(x(k+1)))P(k)\varphi(\tau(x(k+1)))}, \\ P(k+1) = P(k) - \dfrac{P(k)\varphi(\tau(x(k+1))))\varphi^T(\tau(x(k+1)))P(k)}{1+\varphi^T(\tau(x(k+1)))P(k)\varphi(\tau(x(k+1)))} \end{cases} \quad (40)$$

(here $P(k)$ is a covariance matrix) that has filtering ability, or speed-optimal one-step gradient additive-multiplicative Kaczmarz algorithm [39]

$$w(k+1) = w(k) + \lambda_w \frac{y(k+1) - w^T(k)\varphi(\tau(x(k+1)))}{\eta_w + \| \varphi(\tau(x(k+1))) \|}\varphi(\tau(x(k+1))) \quad (41)$$

(here, $0 < \lambda_w < 2$ is a relaxation parameter; $0 \leq \eta_w \leq 1$ is a regularization parameter) that has tracking ability and (given $\lambda_w = 1$, $\eta_w = 0$) the highest performance, or Goodwin-Ramadge-Caines algorithm

$$\begin{cases} w(k+1) = w(k) + r^{-1}(k+1)(y(k+1) - w^T(k)\varphi(\tau(x(k+1))))\varphi(\tau(x(k+1))), \\ r(k+1) = r(k) + \| \varphi(\tau(x(k+1))) \|^2 \end{cases} \quad (42)$$

that is actually stochastic approximation procedure.

In order to adjust parameters of wavelons (vector of centers c_j, receptive fields matrices Q_j^{-1}, shape parameter α_j), we will use gradient minimization of local criterion

$$E(k) = \frac{1}{2}e^2(k) = \frac{1}{2}(y(k) - \hat{y}(k))^2, \quad (43)$$

besides, in contrast to component-wise learning, we will do adjustment in vector-matrix form that, in the first place, is simpler from computational point of view, and, in the second place, will allow of optimizing performance of learning process.

In general case, the learning method can be written as follows:

$$\begin{cases} c_j(k+1) = c_j(k) - \eta_{c_j} \nabla_{c_j} E(k), \\ Q_j^{-1}(k+1) = Q_j^{-1}(k) - \eta_{Q_j^{-1}} \left\{ \dfrac{\partial E(k)}{\partial Q_j^{-1}} \right\}, \\ \alpha(k+1) = \alpha(k) - \eta_\alpha \nabla_\alpha E(k), \ j = 1, 2 \ldots, h \end{cases} \tag{44}$$

where $\nabla_{c_j} E$, $\nabla_\alpha E$ are gradient $(n \times 1)$-vectors of criterion (43) subject to c_j and α correspondingly; $\alpha(k) = (\alpha_1(k), \alpha_2(k), \ldots, \alpha_h(k))^T$ is $(h \times 1)$-vector of adaptive wavelet activation-membership functions shape parameters; $\left\{ \dfrac{\partial E(k)}{\partial Q_j^{-1}} \right\}$ is $(n \times n)$-matrix formed by partial derivatives E subject to components Q_j^{-1}; η_{c_j}, $\eta_{Q_j^{-1}}$ and η_α is a learning rate parameters.

Components of learning method can be written in the following form for adaptive wavelet activation membership function:

$$\begin{cases} \nabla_{c_j} E(k) = 2e(k) w_j(k) Q_j^{-1}(k)(x(k) - c_j(k)) \cdot \\ \cdot(\alpha_j(k)\tau_j^3(x(k)) - (2\alpha_j(k)+1)\tau_j(x(k))) \exp -\tau_j^2(x(k))/2 = e(k) J_{c_j}(k), \\ \{\partial E(k) / \partial Q_j^{-1}\} = -e(k) w_j(k)(x(k) - c_j(k))(x(k) - c_j(k))^T \cdot \\ \cdot(\alpha_j(k)\tau_j^3(x(k)) - (2\alpha_j(k)+1)\tau_j(x(k))) \exp(-\tau_j^2(x(k))/2) = e(k) J_{Q_j^{-1}}(k), \\ \partial E(k) / \partial \alpha = -e(k) w(k) \odot \tau^2(x(k)) \odot \exp\left(-\tau_j^2(x(k))/2\right) - e(k) J_\alpha(k). \end{cases} \tag{45}$$

Hence learning method of W-neurons hidden layer parameters with respect to (44) takes form

$$\begin{cases} c_j(k+1) = c_j(k) - \eta_{c_j} e(k+1) 2 w_j(k+1) Q_j^{-1}(k+1)(x(k+1) - c_j(k+1)) \times \\ \times(\alpha_j(k+1)\tau_j^3(x(k+1)) - (2\alpha_j(k+1)+1)\tau_j(x(k+1))) \exp\left(-\dfrac{\tau_j^2(x(k+1))}{2}\right) = \\ = c_j(k) - \eta_{c_j} e(k+1) J_{c_j}(k+1), \\ Q_j^{-1}(k+1) = Q_j^{-1}(k) + \eta_{Q_j} e(k+1) w_j(k+1)(x(k+1) - c_j(k+1)) \times \\ \times(x(k+1) - c_j(k+1))^T (\alpha_j(k+1)\tau_j^3(x(k+1)) - \\ -(2\alpha_j(k+1)+1)\tau_j(x(k+1))) \exp\left(-\dfrac{\tau_j^2(x(k+1))}{2}\right) = \\ = Q_j^{-1}(k) + \eta_{Q_j} e(k+1) J_{Q_j^{-1}}(k+1), \\ \alpha(k+1) = \alpha(k) + \eta_\alpha e(k+1) w(k+1) \odot \tau^2(x(k+1)) \odot \exp\left(-\dfrac{\tau_j^2(x(k+1))}{2}\right) = \\ = \alpha(k) + \eta_\alpha e(k+1) J_\alpha(k+1) \end{cases} \tag{46}$$

where $\odot$ is a symbol of direct product; $\alpha(k) = (\alpha_1(k), \ldots, \alpha_h(k))^T$; $w(k) = (w_1(k), \ldots, w_h(k))^T$; $\tau(x(k)) = (\tau_1(x(k)), \ldots, \tau_h(x(k)))^T$; $\tau^2(x(k)) = \tau(x(k)) \odot \tau(x(k))$. At that, speed of convergence to optimal values $c_j(k)$, $Q_j^{-1}(k)$ and $\alpha(k)$ is completely defined by step parameters η_{c_j}, $\eta_{Q_j^{-1}}$ and η_α.

In order to increase learning algorithm convergence speed, we will write it in form

$$\begin{cases} c_j(k+1) = c_j(k) - \lambda_c (J_{c_j}(k+1) J_{c_j}^T(k+1) + \eta_{c_j} \mathbf{I})^{-1} J_{c_j}(k+1) e(k+1), \\ \alpha(k+1) = \alpha(k) + \lambda_\alpha (J_\alpha(k+1) J_\alpha^T(k+1) + \eta_\alpha \mathbf{I})^{-1} J_\alpha(k+1) e(k+1) \end{cases} \tag{47}$$

where $\mathbf{I}$ is $(n \times n)$-unity matrix; λ_c, λ_α are positive damping parameters.

Using matrix inversion lemma, after simple transformations, we can obtain simple and effective learning method of centers vector c_j and shape parameters α of W-neuron in form

$$\begin{cases} c_j(k+1) = c_j(k) - \lambda_c \dfrac{e(k+1)J_{c_j}(k+1)}{\eta_{c_j} + \| J_{c_j}(k+1) \|^2}, \\ \alpha(k+1) = \alpha(k) + \lambda_\alpha \dfrac{e(k+1)J_\alpha(k+1)}{\eta_\alpha + \| J_\alpha(k+1) \|^2} \end{cases} \tag{48}$$

that coincides with optimal Kaczmarz-Widrow-Hoff algorithm subject to performance (given $\lambda_c = 1, \eta_{c_j} = 0$, $\lambda_\alpha = 1, \eta_{\alpha_j} = 0$) with an accuracy of notation.

In order to adjust $Q_j^{-1}(k)$, we can use matrix modification of method (48) in form

$$Q_j^{-1}(k+1) = Q_j^{-1}(k) + \lambda_Q \frac{e(k+1)J_{Q_j^{-1}}(k+1)}{\eta_{Q_j^{-1}} + Tr\left(J_{Q_j^{-1}}^T(k+1) J_{Q_j^{-1}}(k+1) \right)} \tag{49}$$

where $\lambda_Q, \eta_{Q_j^{-1}}$ have the same sense that corresponding parameters in (48).

Thus, finally learning method of W-neurons in optimal subject to performance version can be written as

$$\begin{cases} c_j(k+1) = c_j(k) - \dfrac{e(k+1)J_{c_j}(k+1)}{\| J_{c_j}(k+1) \|^2}, \\ Q_j^{-1}(k+1) = Q_j^{-1}(k) + \dfrac{e(k+1)J_{Q_j^{-1}}(k+1)}{Tr\left(J_{Q_j^{-1}}^T(k+1) J_{Q_j^{-1}}(k+1) \right)}, \\ \alpha(k+1) = \alpha(k) + \dfrac{e(k+1)J_\alpha(k+1)}{\| J_\alpha(k+1) \|^2}), \quad j = 1, 2, \ldots, h. \end{cases} \tag{50}$$

It is known that one-step Kaczmarz's algorithm, having high performance, does not have filtering ability, i.e., its performance decreases under intensive perturbations and noises. In order to improve smoothing ability to the learning process, using approach described in [25], one can introduce the following learning procedure:

$$\begin{cases} c_j(k+1) = c_j(k) - \lambda_c(e(k+1)J_{c_j}(k+1)) / \eta_{c_j}(k+1), \\ \eta_{c_j}(k+1) = \beta_c \eta_{c_j}(k) + \| J_{c_j}(k+1) \|^2, \\ Q_j^{-1}(k+1) = Q_j^{-1}(k) + \lambda_Q(e(k+1)J_{Q_j^{-1}}(k+1)) / \eta_{Q_j^{-1}}(k+1), \\ \eta_{Q_j^{-1}}(k+1) = \beta_Q \eta_{Q_j^{-1}}(k) + Tr(J^T_{Q_j^{-1}}(k+1)J_{Q_j^{-1}}(k+1)), \\ \alpha(k+1) = \alpha(k) + \lambda_\alpha(e(k+1)J_\alpha(k+1)) / \eta_\alpha(k+1), \\ \eta_\alpha(k+1) = \beta_\alpha \eta_\alpha(k) + \| J_\alpha(k+1) \|^2, \quad j = 1,2,\ldots,h \end{cases} \tag{51}$$

(here $0 \le \beta_c \le 1$, $0 \le \beta_Q \le 1$, $0 \le \beta_\alpha \le 1$ are forgetting parameters) that is nonlinear hybrid of Kaczmarz-Widrow-Hoff algorithm and Goodwin-Ranadge-Caines algorithm and has both tracking and filtering abilities.

The experience shows that the identification methods based on the least squares criterion are extremely sensitive to the deviation of real data distribution law from Gaussian distribution. In presence of various type outliers, an outrage errors, and non-Gaussian disturbances with "heavy tails" the methods based on the least squares criterion lose their efficiency. In this case the methods of robust estimation and identification which have obtained the wide spread for the learning of the artificial neural networks appear on the first role.

Let us introduce modified robust identification criterion in the form

$$E_R(k) = 1 - \exp(-\delta e^2(k)) \tag{52}$$

where $e(k)$ is learning error, $e(k) = (y(k) - \hat{y}(k)) = y(k) - w^T(k-1)\varphi(\tau(x(k)))$; δ is a positive parameters that is chosen empirically and define size of dead zone regarding bursts. Comparison of robust identification criterion with various parameters δ and least squares criterion is shown in Figure 12.

We use gradient minimization of robust criterion (52) to adjust synaptic weights w and parameters of adaptive wavelet activation-membership functions (vectors c_j, matrices Q_j^{-1}, vector α), at that, in contrast to component-wise learning, we realize adjustment in vector-matrix form that, in the first place, is simpler from computational point of view, and, in the second place, allows optimizing performance of learning.

We can write for multidimensional wavelet activation-membership function $\varphi_j((x(k)-c_j(k))^T Q_j^{-1}(x(k)-c_j(k))) = \varphi_j(\tau_j(x(k)))$

$$\begin{cases} \nabla_w E^R(k) = -2\delta e(k)\exp(-\delta e^2(k))\varphi(\tau(x(k))) = -\delta e(k)\exp(-\delta e^2(k))J_w(k), \\ \nabla_{c_j} E^R(k) = 4\delta e(k)\exp(-\delta e^2(k))w_j(k)\varphi_j'(\tau_j(x(k)))\cdot \\ \cdot Q_j^{-1}(k)(x(k)-c_j(k)) = \delta e(k)\exp(-\delta e^2(k))J_{c_j}(k), \\ \partial E^R(k)/\partial Q_j^{-1} = -2\delta e(k)\exp(-\delta e^2(k))w_j(k)\varphi_j'(\tau_j(x(k)))\cdot \\ \cdot(x(k)-c_j(k))(x(k)-c_j(k))^T = -\delta e(k)\exp(-\delta e^2(k))J_{Q_j^{-1}}(k), \\ \nabla_\alpha E^R(k) = -2\delta e(k)\exp(-\delta e^2(k))w(k)\odot\nabla_\alpha\varphi(\tau(x(k))) = \\ = -\delta e(k)\exp(-\delta e^2(k))J_\alpha(k) \end{cases} \tag{53}$$

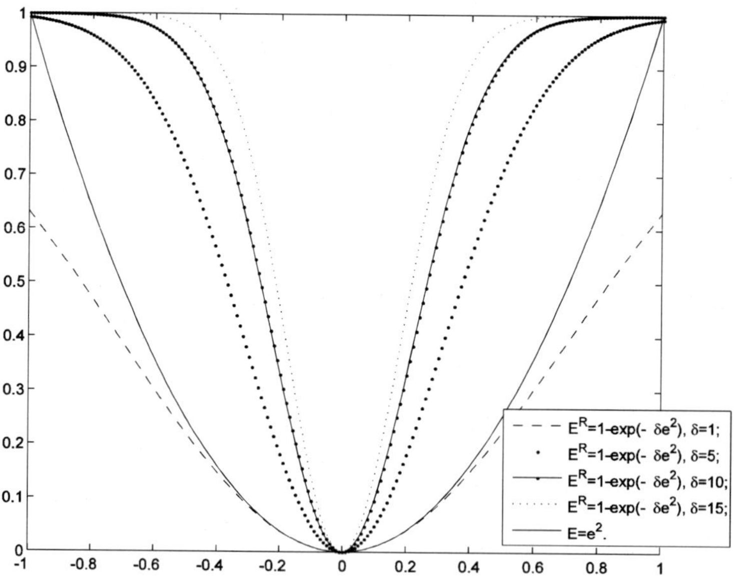

Figure 12. Robust identification criterion (52) with various parameters δ.

where $\varphi_j'(\bullet)$ is a derivative of the j-th wavelet subject to argument $\tau_j(x(k)) = ((x(k) - c_j(k))^T Q_j^{-1}(x(k) - c_j(k)))$.

Hence the learning method of W-neurons with respect to (53) takes form

$$\begin{cases} w(k+1) = w(k) + \eta_w \delta e(k+1)\exp(-\delta e^2(k+1))J_w(k+1), \\ c_j(k+1) = c_j(k) - \eta_{c_j} \delta e(k+1)\exp(-\delta e^2(k+1))J_{c_j}(k+1), \\ Q_j^{-1}(k+1) = Q_j^{-1}(k) + \eta_{Q_j^{-1}} \delta e(k+1)\exp(-\delta e^2(k+1))J_{Q_j^{-1}}(k+1), \\ \alpha(k+1) = \alpha(k) + \eta_\alpha \delta e(k+1)\exp(-\delta e^2(k+1))J_\alpha(k+1). \end{cases} \tag{54}$$

After performing set of simple transformations, we can write robust learning algorithm that is analogous to the algorithm (51) [40, 41]:

$$\begin{cases} w(k+1) = w(k) + \lambda_w(\delta e(k+1)\exp(-\delta e^2(k+1))J_w(k+1)) / \eta_w(k+1), \\ \eta_w(k+1) = \beta_w \eta_w(k) + \| J_w(k+1) \|^2, \\ c_j(k+1) = c_j(k) - \lambda_{c_j}(\delta e(k+1)\exp(-\delta e^2(k+1))J_{c_j}(k+1)) / \eta_{c_j}(k+1), \\ \eta_{c_j}(k+1) = \beta_{c_j}\eta_{c_j}(k) + \| J_{c_j}(k+1) \|^2, \\ Q_j^{-1}(k+1) = Q_j^{-1}(k) + \lambda_{Q_j^{-1}}(\delta e(k+1)\exp(-\delta e^2(k+1))J_{Q_j^{-1}}(k+1)) / \eta_{Q_j^{-1}}(k+1), \\ \eta_{Q_j^{-1}}(k+1) = \beta_{Q_j^{-1}}\eta_{Q_j^{-1}}(k) + Tr(J_{Q_j^{-1}}^T(k+1)J_{Q_j^{-1}}(k+1)), \\ \alpha(k+1) = \alpha(k) + \lambda_\alpha(\delta e(k+1)\exp(-\delta e^2(k+1))J_\alpha(k+1)) / \eta_\alpha(k+1), \\ \eta_\alpha(k+1) = \beta_\alpha \eta_\alpha(k) + \| J_\alpha(k+1) \|^2. \end{cases} \tag{55}$$

WAVELET-NEURO-FUZZY SYSTEMS AND THEIR LEARNING IN TASKS OF DYNAMIC DATA MINING AND INFORMATION PROCESSING

Next step in development of hybrid neural systems is combining of transparency and interpretability of fuzzy inference systems, powerful approximation ability and learnability of artificial neural networks, and compactness and flexibility of wavelet transform into hybrid systems of computational intelligence that will be referred to as adaptive wavelet-neuro-fuzzy network.

The key parameter that defines efficiency of such type systems is a learning method that is mostly based on gradient procedures of the considered criterion minimization. Combination of gradient optimization with error back propagation leads to slow learning process of hybrid system and necessity to use large volume training sets. In case when data processing should be performed in real time, and the set being forecasted is non-stationary and contains noise, conventional gradient algorithms appear to be ineffective.

Let us consider synthesis of one-dimensional and multidimensional adaptive wavelet-neuro-fuzzy system with linear consequent and based on W-neuron as well as their learning methods based on quasi-Newtonian and robust methods that have high performance as compared to systems that use conventional gradient procedures of back propagation.

Such system allows of performing data mining of non-stationary nonlinear time series in sequential mode with consideration that user of the system will not need to choose form and shape of activation functions, and the system will adjust parameters of adaptive wavelet activation-membership function itself during data processing.

Adaptive Neuro-Fuzzy Systems and Their Learning

Generalized learning algorithm of fuzzy inference in Takagi-Sugeno-Kang model with m rules and n variables x_i can be presented as follows:

$$\begin{aligned}
&IF\,(x_1\ is\ A_1^{(1)})\,and \ldots and\,(x_n\ is\ A_n^{(1)})\,THEN\ y_1 = p_{10} + \sum_{i=1}^{n} p_{1i} x_i,\\
&IF\,(x_1\ is\ A_1^{(2)})\,and \ldots and\,(x_n\ is\ A_n^{(2)})\,THEN\ y_2 = p_{20} + \sum_{i=1}^{n} p_{2i} x_i,\\
&\ldots\ldots\ldots\ldots\ldots\\
&IF\,(x_1\ is\ A_1^{(m)})\,and \ldots and\,(x_n\ is\ A_n^{(m)})\,THEN\ y_m = p_{m0} + \sum_{i=1}^{m} p_{mi} x_i.
\end{aligned} \tag{56}$$

Rules (56) are implemented by membership functions that are presented mostly by a Gaussians for each variable x_i

$$\mu_A(x_i) = \exp\left(-\frac{(x_i - c_i)^2}{2\sigma_i^2}\right), \tag{57}$$

where $\mu_A(x_i)$ presents operator A.

In fuzzy networks, it makes sense to set that condition in form of algebraic product that allows of resenting membership function for inference rules in form

$$\mu_A^{(j)}(x) = \prod_{i=1}^{n} \exp\left(-\frac{(x_i - c_i^{(j)})^2}{2(\sigma_i^{(j)})^2}\right). \tag{58}$$

Given m inference rules, output result aggregation is performed regarding to expression

$$\hat{y}(x) = \sum_{j=1}^{m} g_j y_j(x) \bigg/ \sum_{j=1}^{m} g_j \tag{59}$$

where $\hat{y}_j(x) = p_{j0} + \sum_{i=1}^{n} p_{ji} x_i$ (in this case, we obtain 1-order Takagi-Sugeno-Kang system). At that, expression (59) may correspond to architecture of maltilayered neuro-fuzzy system that is shown in Figure 13. Such network contains five layers.

The first layer performs fuzzyfication of each variable x_i $(i = 1, \ldots, N)$ separately, determining value of membership function $\mu_A^j(x_i)$ for each j-th rule. Parameters $c_i^{(j)}, \sigma_i^{(j)}$ of membership function (57) should be adapted during learning.

The second hidden layer aggregates separate variables x_i, determining the resultant value of membership coefficient $g_k = \mu_A^{(j)}(x)$ for vector x (activation level of inference rule) in accordance to expression (58). This layer is nonparametric.

The third hidden layer is a generator of consequent function of such network that calculates polynomial function $\hat{y}_j(x) = p_{j0} + \sum_{i=1}^{n} p_{ji} x_i$ values. Formed in the previous layer, signal $\hat{y}_j(x)$ multiplies g_j in this layer. The layer is parametric, its linear weights p_{ji} $(j=1,2,\ldots,m; i=1,2,\ldots,n)$ determine consequent function in Takagi-Sugeno-Kang neuro-fuzzy network.

The fourth layer consists of two summators one of which calculates weighted sum of signals $\hat{y}_j(x)$, and the second one determines sum of weights $\sum_{j=1}^{m} g_j$. This layer is nonparametric.

The last, fifth layer that consists of the only output neuron is normalizing layer where weights are normalized according to expression (59). Output signal $\hat{y}(x)$ is defined by the expression

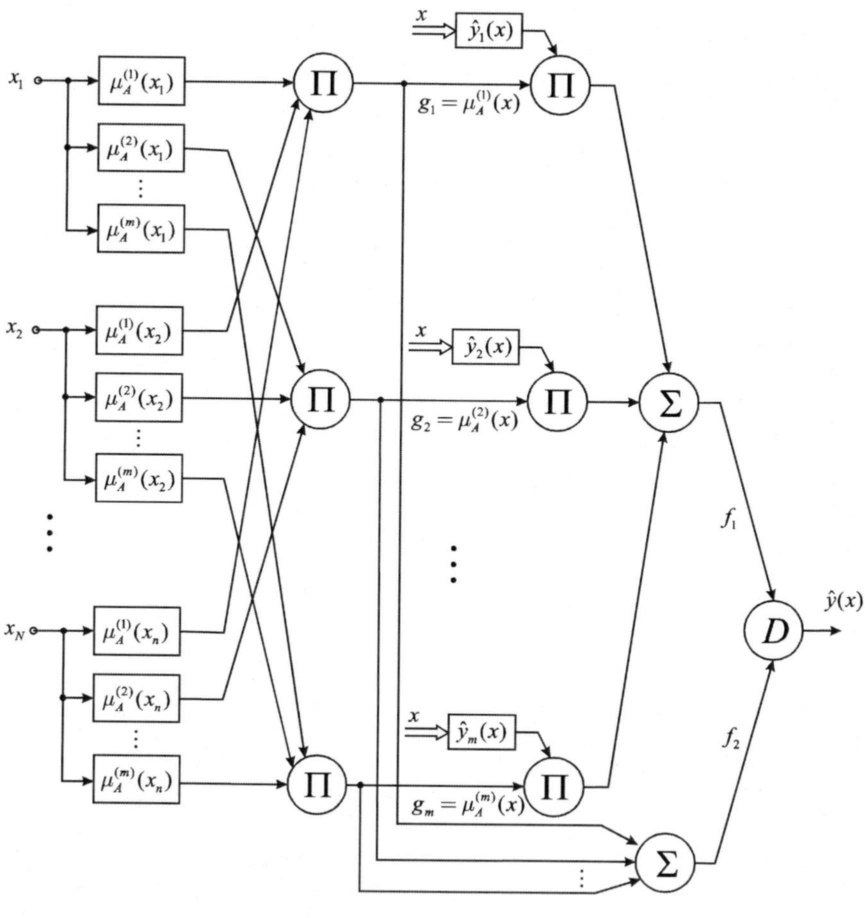

Figure 13. Architecture of Takagi-Sugeno-Kang neuro-fuzzy network.

$$\hat{y}(x) = f(x) = f_1 / f_2. \tag{60}$$

This layer is also nonparametric.

From the description stated above, it follows that Takagi-Sugeno-Kang neuro-fuzzy network contains two parametric layers only (the first one and the third one) whose parameters are adjusted during learning. The first layer parameters are nonlinear since they relate to nonlinear membership function, and the third layer parameters are formed by linear weights as they relate to linear consequent function.

When determining functional dependence of (59) for Takagi-Sugeno-Kang neuro-fuzzy network, we obtain the expression of the following form

$$\hat{y}(x) = \frac{1}{\sum_{j=1}^{m}\prod_{i=1}^{n}\mu_A^{(j)}(x_i)} \sum_{j=1}^{m}\prod_{i=1}^{n}\mu_A^{(j)}(x_i)\left(p_{j0} + \sum_{i=1}^{n} p_{ji}x_i\right). \tag{61}$$

If we consider that condition parameters are fixed at a certain time, the function $\hat{y}(k)$ is a linear function relatively of the variables x_i.

Given n input variables, each rule forms $(n+1)$ parameters p_{ji} of linear consequent. Given m inference rules, this yields $m(n+1)$ linear parameters of network. In tern, each of membership functions uses two parameters (c, σ) that should be adapted. If we consider each variable x_i is determined by its own membership function, then, given m inference rules, we will obtain $3mn$ nonlinear parameters. In total, it yields $m(4n+1)$ linear and nonlinear parameters whose values should be adjusted during learning of neuro-fuzzy network.

In order to decrease number of adjustable parameters in practice, it operates with lesser number of independent membership functions for separate variables, following rules where membership function of different variables are combined.

Let us consider subsequently structure of neuro-fuzzy network that is based on Mamdani-Zadeh fuzzy inference. Such architecture was proposed by L Wang and J. Mendel [42] and consists of four layers. The first layer performs fuzzyfication of input variables, the second one aggregates values of condition activation, the third (linear) one aggregates m inference rules (the first neuron) and generates normalizing signal (the second neuron), whereas one neuron-output layer performs normalization, forming output signal $y(k)$. The first and the third layers only are parametric: these are parameters of membership functions ($c_i^{(j)}, \sigma_i^{(j)}$) in the first layer, and weights $p_1, p_2, \ldots, p_m$ that are treated as the k-th fuzzy inference rule consequent membership function center.

Output of such system is determined by expression of the form

$$\hat{y}(x) = \frac{1}{\sum_{j=1}^{m} \prod_{i=1}^{n} \mu_A^{(j)}(x_i)} \sum_{j=1}^{m} p_j \prod_{i=1}^{n} \mu_A^{(j)}(x_i). \tag{62}$$

Architecture of Wang-Mendel neuro-fuzzy network is shown in Figure 14.

Similarity of structures of both considered neuro-fuzzy networks should be noted. Parts that determine antecedents – the first and the second layer – are identical, and as for consequent, polynomial functions are used in Takagi-Sugeno-Kang neuro-fuzzy system, and scalars that can be treated as zero-order polynomial functions are used in Wang-Mendel neuro-fuzzy network. Thus, from functional point of view, Wang-Mendel network is similar to Takagi-Sugeno-Kang neuro-fuzzy network, or, speaking more specifically, it is its particular case.

The task of both neuro-fuzzy networks is to perform such mapping of pairs of data (x, y) so that expected value that corresponds to input vector x is formed by output network function $\hat{y}(x)$. In spite of the considered neuro-fuzzy networks have one output only, they can be generalized for the case of system with several outputs.

Similar to conventional neural networks, neuro-fuzzy networks learning can be performed according to supervised algorithm that is based on goal function minimization that is defined, as a rule, using the Euclidean norm

$$E = \frac{1}{2} \sum_{k=1}^{N_s} \quad y(k) - \hat{y}(k) \quad ^2 \tag{63}$$

where N_s is a amount of data in training set.

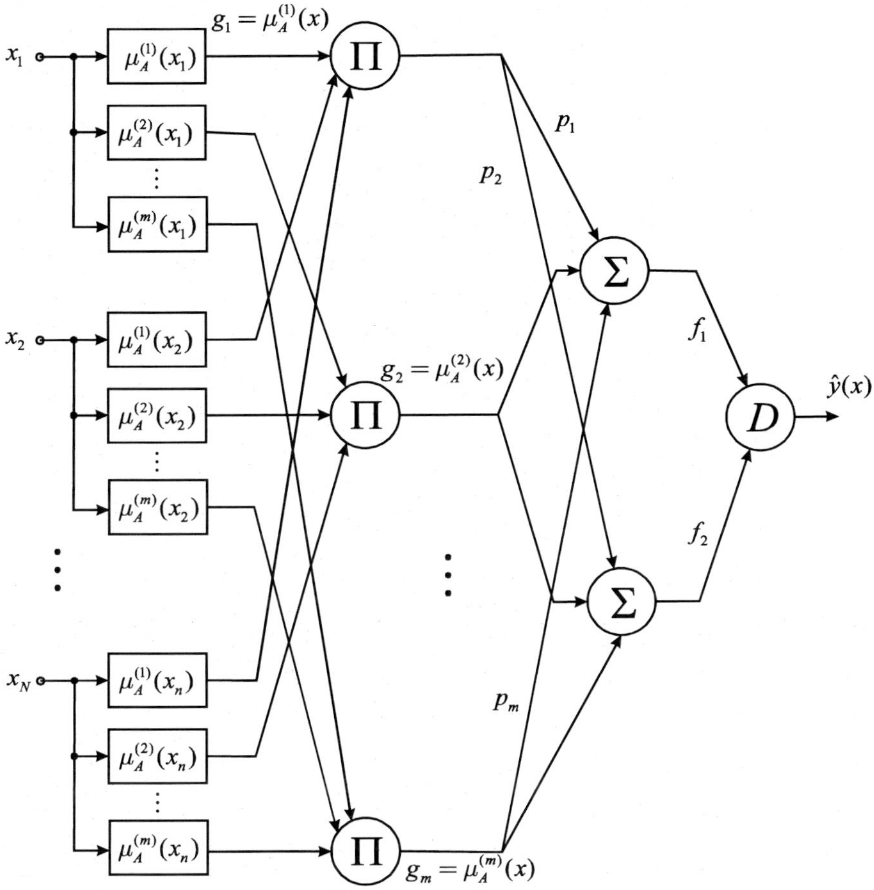

Figure 14. Architecture of Wang-Mendel neuro-fuzzy network.

Along with advantages, neuro-fuzzy systems have also shortcomings, namely, strict set of shape and parameters of membership function, inability to process non-stationary signals with rapidly changing structure, increase of power of polynomial function that leads to loss of extrapolating ability. In order to extend functional abilities of neuro-fuzzy networks, design of hybrid wavelet-neuro-fuzzy systems with adaptive wavelet activation-membership functions it topical problem.

Adaptive Wavelet-Neuro-Fuzzy Network with Linear Consequent and One-Dimensional Adaptive Wavelet Activation-Membership Functions in Hidden Layer and Its Learning Method

Let us consider five-layer architecture [43] that is shown in Figure 15a, or in Figure 16a is similar to known adaptive neuro-fuzzy system (ANFIS) that is, in turn, learnable Takagi-Sugeno-Kang fuzzy inference system discussed above.

There are two possible cases of input space partitioning: Figure 15b presents grid partitioning of input space, and Figure 16b presents scatter partitioning of input space for two-inputs adaptive wavelet-neuro-fuzzy network.

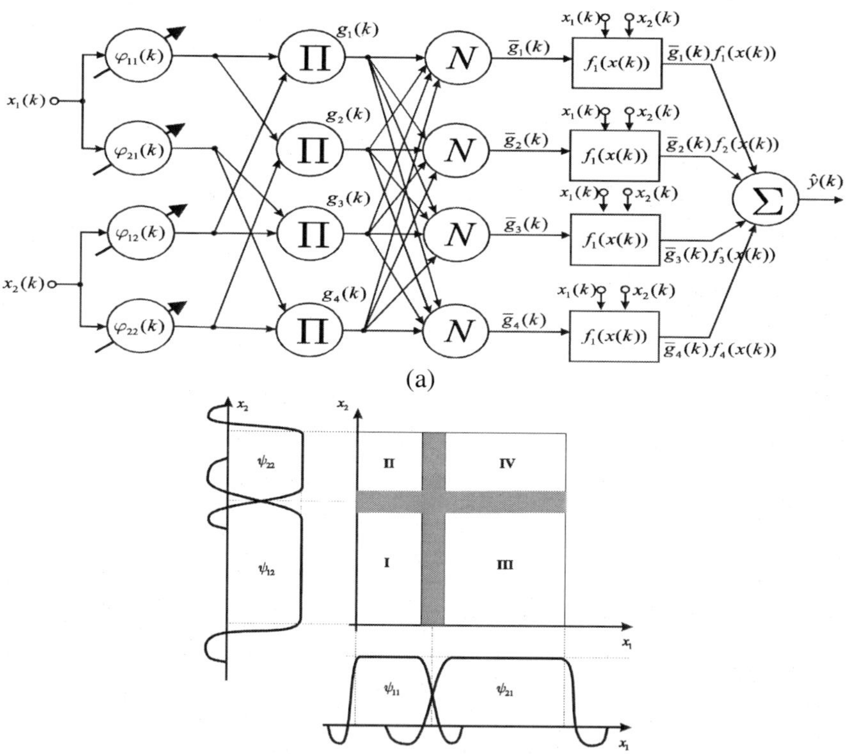

Figure 15. Adaptive wavelet-neuro-fuzzy network with grid partitioning of input space: a – network architecture, b – wavelet activation-membership functions and activation rules plane.

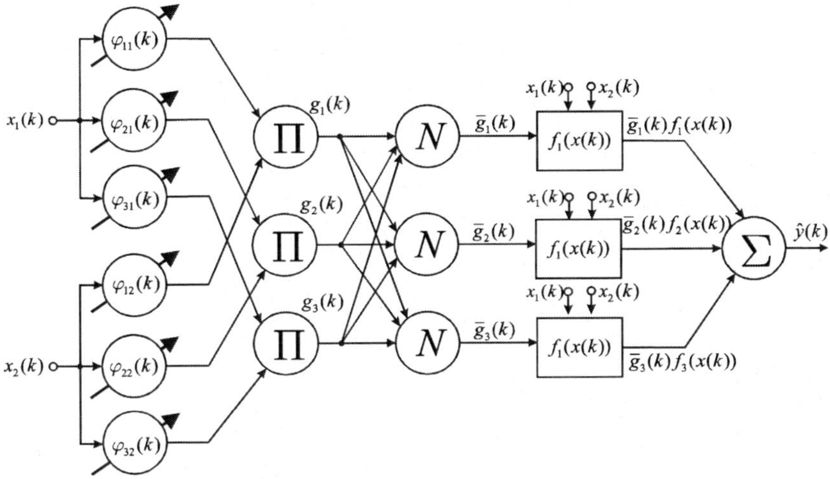

(a)

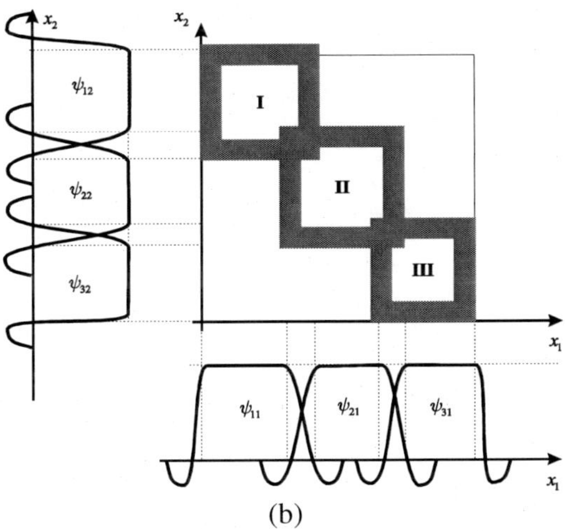

(b)

Figure 16. Adaptive wavelet-neuro-fuzzy network with scatter partitioning of input space: a – network architecture; b – wavelet activation-membership functions and activation rules plane.

Let us consider architecture of adaptive wavelet-neuro-fuzzy network with scatter dispersed partitioning in general form as it, having universal approximation ability, has less number of adjustable parameters. Its architecture is shown in Figure 17.

The zeroth layer of the architecture is receptive and at a instant time k it receives input signal in form of vector $x(k)=(x_1(k),x_2(k),\ldots,x_n(k))^T$. In cases of time series forecasting, the layer can be formed by delay units z^{-1} $(z^{-1}x(k)=x(k-1))$ so when signal $x(k)$ appears on its input, its output forms vector of history $x(k)=(x(k-1),x(k-2),\ldots,x(k-n))^T$.

The first hidden layer, in contrast to neuro-fuzzy systems, consists not of conventional non-negative membership functions, but of set of hn wavelets (h wavelets per each input) $\psi_{ji}(x_i)=\psi_{ji}(x_i,c_{ji}^{\psi},\sigma_{ji})$ with $2hn$ adjustable parameters of centers c_{ji}^{ψ} and widths σ_{ji}.

The second hidden layer performs operation that is similar to obtaining fuzzy T-norm

$$g_j(k)=\prod_{i=1}^{n}\psi_{ji}(x_i(k)),\quad j=1,2,\ldots,h, \tag{64}$$

after that, normalization takes place in the third hidden layer

$$\bar{g}_j(k)=\frac{g_j(k)}{\sum_{j=1}^{h}g_j(k)}=\frac{\prod_{i=1}^{n}\psi_{ji}(x_i(k))}{\sum_{j=1}^{h}\prod_{i=1}^{n}\psi_{ji}(x_i(k))} \tag{65}$$

that ensures the following condition satisfaction:

$$\sum_{j=1}^{h}\bar{g}_j(k)=1. \tag{66}$$

The fourth hidden layer performs operation that is similar to obtaining consequent in fuzzy inference systems $\bar{g}_j(k)f_j(x(k))$, at that, as a function $f_j(x(k))$, it is mostly used linear form

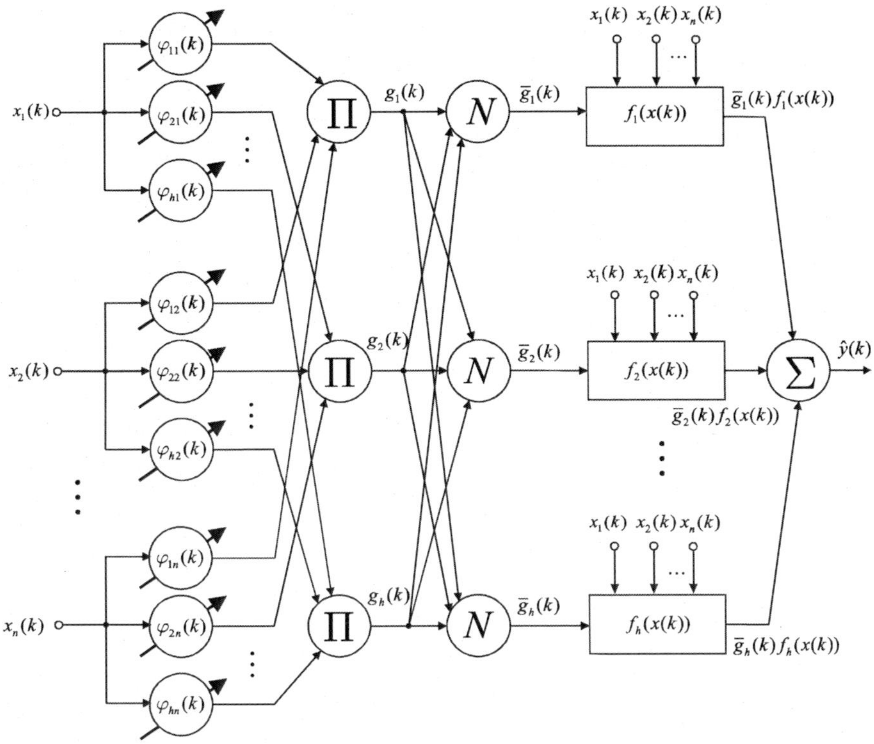

Figure 17. Architecture of wavelet-neuro-fuzzy network with linear consequent.

$$f_j(x(k)) = p_{j0} + \sum_{i=1}^{n} p_{ji} x_i(k). \tag{67}$$

In this case, signal values are calculated in the fourth hidden layer as follows:

$$\bar{g}_j(k)\left(p_{j0} + \sum_{i=1}^{n} p_{ji} x_i(k)\right) = \bar{g}_j(k) p_j^T \bar{x}(k) \tag{68}$$

where $\bar{x}(k) = (1, x^T(k))^T$; $p_j = (p_{j0}, p_{j1}, \ldots, p_{jn})^T$.

Thus, $h(n+1)$ parameters p_{ji}, ($j = 1, 2, \ldots, h$, $i = 0, 1, 2, \ldots, n$) should be determined.

And, finally, in the fifth hidden layer, the output signal

$$\begin{aligned}\hat{y}(k) &= \sum_{j=1}^{h}\bar{g}_j(k)f_j(x(k)) = \sum_{j=1}^{h}\frac{g_j(k)}{\sum_{j=1}^{h}g_j(k)}f_j(x(k)) = \\ &= \sum_{j=1}^{h}\frac{\prod_{i=1}^{n}\psi_{ji}(x_i(k),c_{ji}^{\psi},\sigma_{ji})}{\sum_{j=1}^{h}\prod_{i=1}^{n}\psi_{ji}(x_i(k),c_{ji}^{\psi},\sigma_{ji})}f_j(x(k))\end{aligned} \tag{69}$$

is calculated that, being based on variables vectors $f(x(k)) = (\bar{g}_1(k), \bar{g}_1(k)x_1(k), \quad \ldots, \bar{g}_1(k)x_n(k), \bar{g}_2(k), \bar{g}_2(k)x_1(k), \ldots, \bar{g}_2(k)x_n(k), \ldots, \bar{g}_h(k), \bar{g}_h(k)x_1(k), \ldots, \bar{g}_h(k)x_n(k))^T$,
$p = (p_{10}, p_{11}, \ldots, p_{1n}, p_{20}, p_{21}, \ldots, p_{2n}, p_{h0}, p_{h1}, \ldots, p_{hn})^T$ of dimensionality $(h(n+1))$, can be expressed in compact form

$$\hat{y}(k) = p^T f(x(k)). \tag{70}$$

Adjustable parameters of the network are contained in the first and fourth hidden layers only. These are $2hn$ parameters of wavelets c_{ji}^{ψ} and σ_{ji} and $h(n+1)$ parameters of linear local models p_{ji}. They are the parameters that should be determined during learning process.

Since required vector of synaptic weights vector is linear in the network model, one can use any algorithm that is used in adaptive identification to adjust it, for example, exponentially weighted recurrent method of least squares in the form

$$\begin{cases} p(k+1) = p(k) + \dfrac{P(k)(y(k+1) - p^T(k)f(x(k+1)))}{\beta + f^T(x(k+1))P(k)f(x(k+1))}f(x(k+1)), \\ P(k+1) = \dfrac{1}{\beta}\left(P(k) - \dfrac{P(k)f(x(k+1))f^T(x(k+1))P(k)}{\beta + f^T(x(k+1))P(k)f(x(k+1))}\right) \end{cases} \tag{71}$$

(here $p^T(k)f(x(k+1)) = \hat{y}(k+1)$, $e(k+1) = y(k+1) - \hat{y}(k+1)$ is forecasting error) that is actually second-order optimization procedure and has both filtering and tracking abilities; performance-wise optimal one-step gradient Kaczmarz algorithm that has tracking ability

$$p(k+1)=p(k)+\frac{y(k+1)-p^T(k)f(x(k+1))}{f^T(x(k+1))f(x(k+1))}f(x(k+1)) \tag{72}$$

or Goodwin-Ramadge-Cainse algorithm [56]

$$\begin{cases} p(k+1)=p(k)+\eta^{-1}(k+1)(y(k+1)-p^T(k)f(x(k+1)))f(x(k+1)), \\ \eta(k+1)=\eta(k)+\| f(x(k+1))\|^2 \end{cases} \tag{73}$$

that is actually stochastic approximation procedure.

In order to adjust the first hidden layer parameters in adaptive wavelet-neuro-fuzzy network, we used modified algorithm of error back propagation that is based on chain rule of differentiating and gradient optimization of local criterion

$$E(k)=\frac{1}{2}e^2(k)=\frac{1}{2}(y(k)-\hat{y}(k)). \tag{74}$$

In general case, this layer parameters learning procedure is

$$\begin{cases} c_{ji}^{\psi}(k+1)=c_{ji}^{\psi}(k)-\eta_{c^{\psi}}(k)(\partial E(k)/\partial c_{ji}^{\psi}(k)), \\ \sigma_{ji}(k+1)=\sigma_{ji}(k)-\eta_{\sigma}(k)(\partial E(k)/\partial \sigma_{ji}(k)) \end{cases} \tag{75}$$

and its properties are fully determined by parameters of step $\eta_{c^{\psi}}(k)$, $\eta_{\sigma}(k)$ that usually are chosen empirically. It makes sense to note that, if the fourth hidden layer can be adjusted as fast as possible, such performance is lost in the first hidden layer.

Let us rewrite the learning algorithm in the generalized form

$$\Psi(k+1)=\Psi(k)+\lambda_{\Psi}(J^{\psi}(k)J^{\psi T}(k)+\eta\mathbf{I})^{-1}J^{\psi}(k)e(k) \tag{76}$$

where $\Psi(k)=(c_{11}^{\psi}(k),\sigma_{11}^{-1}(k),\ldots,c_{ji}^{\psi}(k),\sigma_{ji}^{-1}(k),\ldots,c_{hn}^{\psi}(k),\quad \sigma_{hn}^{-1}(k))$ are $(2hn\times 1)$-vector of adjustable parameters, at that in order to simplify computational implementation, it contains not width parameter σ_{ji}, but its inversed value σ_{ji}^{-1}; $J^{\psi}(k)$ is gradient-$(2hn\times 1)$-vector of output signal $\hat{y}(k)$ subject to adjustable parameters; $\mathbf{I}$ is $(2hn\times 2hn)$-unity matrix.

In order to calculate components of gradient-vector

$$J^{\psi}(k)=\left(\frac{\partial\hat{y}(k)}{\partial c_{11}^{\psi}},\frac{\partial\hat{y}(k)}{\partial\sigma_{11}^{-1}},\ldots,\frac{\partial\hat{y}(k)}{\partial c_{ji}^{\psi}},\frac{\partial\hat{y}(k)}{\partial\sigma_{ji}^{-1}},\ldots,\frac{\partial\hat{y}(k)}{\partial c_{hn}^{\psi}},\frac{\partial\hat{y}(k)}{\partial\sigma_{hn}^{-1}}\right) \tag{77}$$

we used chain rule, at that

$$\begin{cases}\dfrac{\partial\hat{y}(k)}{\partial c_{ji}^{\psi}}=\dfrac{\partial\hat{y}(k)}{\partial\bar{g}_j}\cdot\dfrac{\partial\bar{g}_j}{\partial g_j}\cdot\dfrac{\partial g_j}{\partial\psi_{ji}}\cdot\dfrac{\partial\psi_{ji}}{\partial c_{ji}^{\psi}}=\dfrac{f_j(x(k))\bar{g}_j(k)(1-\bar{g}_j(k))}{\psi_{ji}(x_i(k),c_{ji}^{\psi},\sigma_{ji}^{-1})}\cdot\dfrac{\partial\psi_{ji}}{\partial c_{ji}^{\psi}},\\[2ex] \dfrac{\partial\hat{y}(k)}{\partial\sigma_{ji}^{-1}}=\dfrac{\partial\hat{y}(k)}{\partial\bar{g}_j}\cdot\dfrac{\partial\bar{g}_j}{\partial g_j}\cdot\dfrac{\partial g_j}{\partial\psi_{ji}}\cdot\dfrac{\partial\psi_{ji}}{\partial\sigma_{ji}^{-1}}=\dfrac{f_j(x(k))\bar{g}_j(k)(1-\bar{g}_j(k))}{\psi_{ji}(x_i(k),c_{ji},\sigma_{ji}^{-1})}\cdot\dfrac{\partial\psi_{ji}}{\partial\sigma_{ji}^{-1}}.\end{cases} \tag{78}$$

In order to simplify computational complexity of the learning algorithm, one can use inverse matrix lemma in the form

$$(J^{\psi}J^{\psi T}+\eta\mathbf{I})^{-1}=\eta^{-1}\mathbf{I}-\frac{\eta\mathbf{I}J^{\psi}J^{\psi T}\eta^{-1}\mathbf{I}}{1+J^{\psi T}\eta^{-1}\mathbf{I}J^{\psi}}, \tag{79}$$

on the base of which it is easy to obtain expression

$$\lambda_{\Psi}(J^{\psi}J^{\psi T}+\eta\mathbf{I})^{-1}J^{\psi}=\lambda_{\Psi}\frac{J^{\psi}}{\eta+\|J^{\psi}\|^2}, \tag{80}$$

substituting to (76), we obtain learning method for parameters in the first hidden layer in form [41]

$$\Psi(k+1)=\Psi(k)+\lambda_{\Psi}\frac{J^{\psi}(k+1)e(k+1)}{\eta+\|J^{\psi}(k+1)\|^2}. \tag{81}$$

It is readily to see that method (81) is nonlinear additive-multiplicative modification of Kaczmarz algorithm, and given $\lambda_\Psi = 1$, $\eta = 0$, is structurally identical to it.

In order to provide filtering ability to method (81), let us introduce an additional procedure of regularization parameter η in the form [43, 46, 45]

$$\begin{cases} \Psi(k+1) = \Psi(k) + \lambda_\Psi \dfrac{J^\psi(k+1)e(k+1)}{\eta(k+1)}, \\ \eta(k+1) = \beta\eta(k) + \| J^\psi(k+1) \|^2, \end{cases} \tag{82}$$

that is identical to (81) when $\beta = 0$ and has maximal convergence rate, and when $\beta = 1$, it reveals stochastic approximation ability and is a generalization of procedure (75) for nonlinear case. It makes sense to note here that method (82) is stable with any values of forgetting parameter β that is an advantage of it over exponentially weighted recurrent method of least squares (70).

In connection with the stated above, it makes sense to use the procedure in the form

$$\begin{cases} p(k+1) = p(k) + \lambda_p \dfrac{x(k+1) - p^T(k) f(x(k+1))}{\eta(k+1)} f(x(k+1)), \\ \eta(k+1) = \beta\eta(k) + \| f(x(k+1)) \|^2 \end{cases} \tag{83}$$

to adjust parameters of the fourth layer. It is possible to notice that methods (70) and (83) are closely related since

$$\eta^{-1}(k) = TrP(k), \tag{84}$$

however (83) is much more simpler in numerical implementation and it can easily reset its abilities from tracking to filtering.

Hybrid Adaptive Wavelet-Neuro-Fuzzy System Based on Adaptive W-Neurons with One-Dimensional Adaptive Wavelet Activation-Membership Functions in Hidden Layer and Its Learning Method

Let us consider five-layered architecture [44, 45] that is shown in Figure 18 and is actually similar to the known adaptive neuro-fuzzy networks and to structure presented in [46, 47] and that is, in general case, hybridized Takagi-Sugeno-Kang fuzzy inference system.

The first hidden layer is formed not by conventional non-negative membership functions, but by set of $h_\psi n$ wavelets with $2h_\psi n$ adjustable parameters of center c_{ji}^{ψ} and width σ_{ji}. In adaptive hybrid wavelet-neuro-fuzzy system, we use the previously proposed in [21] adjustable wavelet activation-membership function that has the following form under considered notation for the network being designed:

$$\begin{aligned} \psi_{ji}(x(k)) &= \left(1-\alpha_{ji}^{\psi}(k)t_{ji}^{2}(x(k))\right)\exp\left(-t_{ji}^{2}(x(k))/2\right), \\ \varphi_{jm}(x(k)) &= \left(1-\alpha_{jm}^{\varphi}(k)\tau_{jm}^{2}(x(k))\right)\exp\left(-\tau_{jm}^{2}(x(k))/2\right) \end{aligned} \tag{85}$$

where $\alpha_{ji}^{\psi},\alpha_{jm}^{\varphi}$ are adjustable shape parameters of function $(0\le\alpha_{ji}^{\psi},\alpha_{jm}^{\varphi}\le 1)$; $t_{ji}(x(k))=\left(x(k)-c_{ji}^{\psi}(k)\right)\sigma_{ji}^{-1}(k)$; $\tau_{jm}(x(k))=\left((x(k)-c_{jm}^{\varphi}(k))^{T}Q_{jm}^{-1}(k)(x(k)-c_{jm}^{\varphi}(k))\right)$.

The second hidden layer performs operation that is similar to calculation of fuzzy T–norm (64), after that, in the third hidden layer, normalization in form of (65) takes place, ensuring condition (66) satisfaction (in this case $j=1,2,\ldots,h_\psi$).

The fourth hidden layer performs operation that is similar to consequent calculation in fuzzy inference systems, at that, instead of linear output functions $f_j(x(k))$, we use structure of adaptive W-neuron (wavelon) [20] that allows of improving approximation ability of the system in tasks of forecasting and extrapolation:

$$f_j(x(k))=w_{j0}(k)+\sum_{m=1}^{h_\varphi}w_{jm}(k)\varphi_{jm}(\tau_{jm}(k))=w_j^{T}(k)\varphi_j(\tau_j(k)) \tag{86}$$

where $\varphi_{j0}=1$; $w_j(k)=\left(w_{j0}(k),\ldots,w_{jh_\varphi}(k)\right)^T$; $\varphi_j(\tau_j(k))=(1,\ \varphi_{j1}(\tau_{j1}(k)),\ldots,$ $\varphi_{jh_\varphi}(\tau_{jh_\varphi}(k)))^T$.

In this case, the following values are calculated in the fourth hidden layer:

$$\bar{g}_j(k)\left(w_{j0}(k)+\sum_{m=1}^{h_\varphi}w_{jm}(\tau_{jm}(k))\right)=\bar{g}_j(k)w_j^T(k)\varphi_j(\tau_j(k)) \tag{87}$$

where $h_\varphi(n+1)$ parameters w_{jm}, $j=1,2,\ldots,h_\varphi$, $m=0,1,2,\ldots,h_\psi$ should be determined.

In the fifth hidden layer, the output signal of the system that can be written in the following form

$$\hat{y}(k)=\bar{g}^T(k)f(x(k)), \tag{88}$$

where $f(x(k))=(w_1^T(k)\varphi_1(\tau_1(k)),\ldots,w_{h_\psi}^T(k)\varphi_{h_\psi}(\tau_{h_\psi}(k)))$.

By substituting variables $F(x(k))=(\bar{g}_1(k)\varphi_1(\tau_1(k)),\ldots,\bar{g}_{h_\psi}(k)\varphi_{h_\psi}(\tau_{h_\psi}(k)))^T$ и $w=(w_1,w_2,\ldots,w_{h_\psi})^T$, we can write output of such architecture in the compact form

$$\hat{y}(k)=w^T(k)F(x(k)). \tag{89}$$

Thus, it can be noted that adjustable parameters are situated in the first and fourth hidden layers. These are $3h_\psi n$ parameters of one-dimensional adaptive wavelet activation-membership function c_{ji}^ψ, σ_{ji} and α_{ji}^ψ; $h_\psi(h_\varphi+1)$ synaptic weights w_{jm}; $h_\psi h_\varphi$ parameters of centers c_{jm}^φ; $h_\psi h_\varphi$ matrices of receptive fields Q_{jm}^{-1} and $h_\psi h_\varphi$ parameters of shape α_{jm}^φ of multidimensional wavelet activation-membership functions of adaptive W-neuron.

Depending on the complexity of the problem being solved and the required accuracy of the solution, it is possible to adjust some parameters of hybrid adaptive wavelet-neuro-fuzzy system at the same time that allows of cutting learning time and of using the system to process short time series.

In order to adjust parameters of the first hidden layer, we use the modified error back propagation algorithm and the gradient optimization method of local criterion

$$E(k)=1/2e^2(k)=1/2(y(k)-\hat{y}(k))^2=1/2(y(k)-w^T(k)F(x(k)))^2. \quad (90)$$

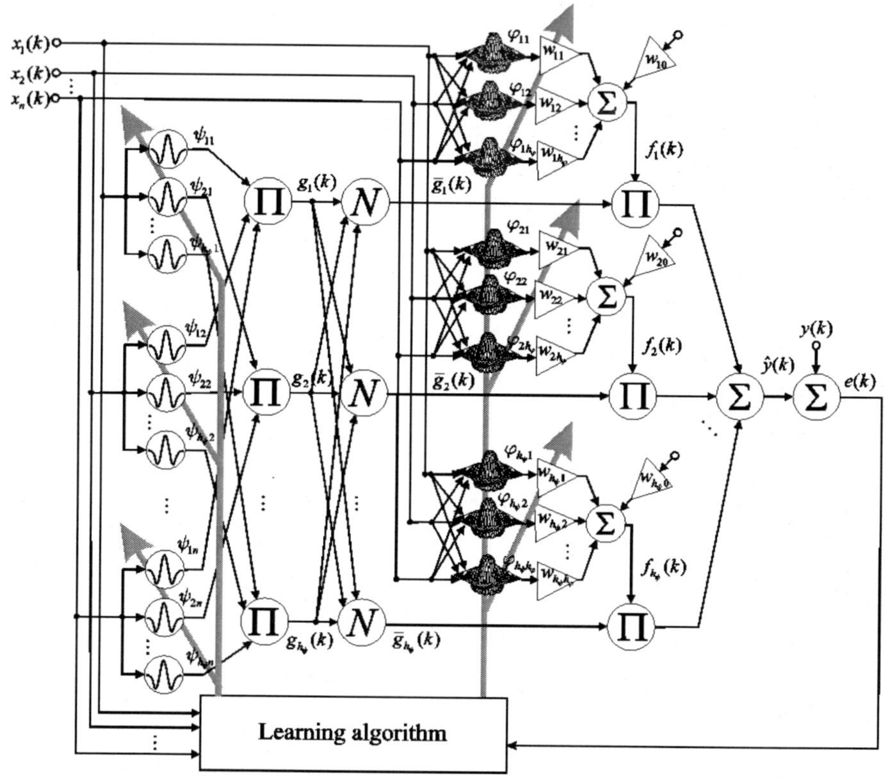

Figure18. Architecture of hybrid adaptive wavelet-neuro-fuzzy system based on adaptive W-neurons with one-dimensional adaptive wavelet activation-membership functions in hidden layer.

In general case, the learning procedure of this layer parameters has the form

$$\begin{cases} c_{ji}^{\psi}(k+1) = c_{ji}^{\psi}(k) - \eta_{c_{ji}^{\psi}} \ \partial E(k) / \partial c_{ji}^{\psi}(k) \ , \\ \sigma_{ji}^{-1}(k+1) = \sigma_{ji}^{-1}(k) - \eta_{\sigma_{ji}^{-1}} \ \partial E(k) / \partial \sigma_{ji}^{-1}(k) \ , \\ \alpha_{ji}^{\psi}(k+1) = \alpha_{ji}^{\psi}(k) - \eta_{c_{ji}^{\psi}} \ \partial E(k) / \partial \alpha_{ji}^{\psi}(k) \end{cases} \tag{91}$$

and its properties are determined by learning rate parameters $\eta_{c_{ji}^{\psi}}$, $\eta_{\sigma_{ji}^{-1}}$, $\eta_{c_{ji}^{\psi}}$.

It is possible to achieve increasing of the convergence speed via usage of procedures in the form (81) where, in this case, vector of adjustable parameters $\Psi(k) = (c_{11}^{\psi}(k), \sigma_{11}^{-1}(k), \alpha_{11}^{\psi}(k), \dots, c_{h_{\psi}n}^{\psi}, \sigma_{h_{\psi}n}^{-1}(k), \alpha_{h_{\psi}n}^{\psi}(k))$ – $(3h_{\psi}n \times 1)$ is extended with one more adjusted parameter; $J^{\psi}(k)$ is gradient-$(3h_{\psi}n \times 1)$-vector of input signal $y(k)$ with respect to adjustable parameters.

In order to obtain components of gradient-vector

$$J^{\psi}(k) = \left(\frac{\partial y(k)}{\partial c_{11}^{\psi}(k)}, \frac{\partial y(k)}{\partial \sigma_{11}^{-1}(k)}, \frac{\partial y(k)}{\partial \alpha_{11}^{\psi}(k)}, \dots, \frac{\partial y(k)}{\partial c_{h_{\psi}n}^{\psi}(k)}, \frac{\partial y(k)}{\partial \sigma_{h_{\psi}n}^{-1}(k)}, \frac{\partial y(k)}{\partial \alpha_{h_{\psi}n}^{\psi}(k)} \right)^{T} \tag{92}$$

we can use expressions in the form

$$\begin{cases} \dfrac{\partial y(k)}{\partial c_{ji}^{\psi}(k)} = \dfrac{f_j(X(k))\bar{g}_j(k)(1-\bar{g}_j(k))}{\psi_{ji}(x_i(k), c_{ji}^{\psi}(k), \sigma_{ji}^{-1}(k), \alpha_{ji}^{\psi})} \cdot \dfrac{\partial \psi_{ji}(x_i(k), c_{ji}^{\psi}(k), \sigma_{ji}^{-1}(k), \alpha_{ji}^{\psi})}{\partial c_{ji}^{\psi}(k)}, \\ \dfrac{\partial y(k)}{\partial \sigma_{ji}^{-1}(k)} = \dfrac{f_j(X(k))\bar{g}_j(k)(1-\bar{g}_j(k))}{\psi_{ji}(x_i(k), c_{ji}^{\psi}(k), \sigma_{ji}^{-1}(k), \alpha_{ji}^{\psi})} \cdot \dfrac{\partial \psi_{ji}(x_i(k), c_{ji}^{\psi}(k), \sigma_{ji}^{-1}(k), \alpha_{ji}^{\psi})}{\partial \sigma_{ji}^{-1}(k)}, \\ \dfrac{\partial y(k)}{\partial \alpha_{ji}^{\psi}(k)} = \dfrac{f_j(X(k))\bar{g}_j(k)(1-\bar{g}_j(k))}{\psi_{ji}(x_i(k), c_{ji}^{\psi}(k), \sigma_{ji}^{-1}(k), \alpha_{ji}^{\psi}))} \cdot \dfrac{\partial \psi_{ji}(x_i(k), c_{ji}^{\psi}(k), \sigma_{ji}^{-1}(k), \alpha_{ji}^{\psi})}{\partial \alpha_{ji}^{\psi}(k)}. \end{cases} \tag{93}$$

Then, performing a set of transformations in form of (79)-(81), we can write learning method of hybrid adaptive wavelet-neuro-fuzzy system based on W-neuron that has filtering and tracking abilities in the following form [40]

$$\begin{cases} \Psi(k+1) = \Psi(k) + \lambda_{\Psi} \dfrac{J^{\Psi}(k+1)e(k+1)}{\eta_{\psi}(k+1)}, \\ \eta(k+1) = \beta\eta_{\Psi}(k) + \| J^{\Psi}(k+1) \|^2 . \end{cases} \tag{94}$$

Let us now consider learning of parameters of the fourth hidden layer, namely, parameters of adaptive W-neuron.

As it was described above, $(h_{\varphi}+1)\times 1$-vector of adjustable synaptic weights w is linear in the network model, thus it can be adjusted with any adaptive identification methods.

In order to adjust parameters of W-neurons (vectors c_j^{φ}, matrices Q_j^{-1}, shape parameters α_j^{φ}) we use gradient minimization of local criterion (90) in the form

$$\begin{cases} c_j^{\varphi}(k+1) = c_j^{\varphi}(k) - \lambda_{c_j^{\varphi}}(e(k+1)J^{\varphi}_{c_j^{\varphi}}(k+1)) / \eta_{c_j^{\varphi}}(k+1), \\ \eta_{c_j^{\varphi}}(k+1) = \gamma_{c_j^{\varphi}}\eta_{c_j^{\varphi}}(k) + \| J^{\varphi}_{c_j^{\varphi}}(k+1) \|^2, \\ Q_j^{-1}(k+1) = Q_j^{-1}(k) + \lambda_{Q_j^{-1}}(e(k+1)J^{\varphi}_{Q_j^{-1}}(k+1)) / \eta_{Q_j^{-1}}(k+1), \\ \eta_{Q_j^{-1}}(k+1) = \gamma_{Q_j^{-1}}\eta_{Q_j^{-1}}(k) + Tr\left(J^{\varphi T}_{Q_j^{-1}}(k+1) J^{\varphi}_{Q_j^{-1}}(k+1) \right), \\ \alpha_j^{\varphi}(k+1) = \alpha_j^{\varphi}(k) + \lambda_{\alpha_j^{\varphi}}(e(k+1)J^{\varphi}_{\alpha_j^{\varphi}}(k+1)) / \eta_{\alpha_j^{\varphi}}(k+1), \\ \eta_{\alpha_j^{\varphi}}(k+1) = \gamma_{\alpha_j^{\varphi}}\eta_{\alpha_j^{\varphi}}(k) + \| J^{\varphi}_{\alpha_j^{\varphi}}(k+1) \|^2 \end{cases} \tag{95}$$

where

$$\begin{cases} J^{\varphi}_{c_j}(k+1) = w_j(k)Q_j^{-1}(k+1)(x(k+1) - c_j^{\varphi}(k+1)) \cdot \\ \cdot\ \alpha_j(k+1)\tau_j^3(x(k+1)) - (2\alpha_j(k+1)+1)\tau_j(x(k+1))\ \exp\ -\tau_j^2(x(k+1))/2\ , \\ J^{-1}_{Q_j}(k+1) = w_j(k)(x(k+1) - c_j^{\varphi}(k+1))(x(k+1) - c_j^{\varphi}(k+1))^T \cdot \\ \cdot\ \alpha_j(k+1)\tau_j^3(x(k+1)) - (2\alpha_j(k+1)+1)\tau_j(x(k+1))\ \exp\left(-\tau_j^2(x(k+1))/2\right), \\ J^{\varphi}_{\alpha_j}(k+1) = w_j(k)\tau_j^2(x(k+1))\exp\left(-\tau_j^2(x(k+1))/2\right). \end{cases} \tag{96}$$

Hybrid Adaptive Wavelet-Neuro-Fuzzy System Based on Adaptive W-Neurons with Adjustable Multidimensional Adaptive Wavelet Activation-Membership Functions in Hidden Layer and Its Learning Method

Let us consider adaptive wavelet-neuro-fuzzy system based on W-neurons that differs from the previously proposed ones by usage of multidimensional wavelet activation-membership functions both in antecedent and in consequent. It makes sense to use such architecture to analyze and process multidimensional nonlinear non-stationary times series.

Architecture of hybrid adaptive wavelet-neuro-fuzzy system based on W-neurons with multidimensional adaptive wavelet activation-membership functions in hidden layer is shown in Figure 19.

The architecture under consideration is a hybrid neuro-fuzzy system that generalizes Takagi-Sugeno-Kang neuro-fuzzy system, Abiyev's fuzzy-wavelet-neural network [46, 47], and multidimensional radial basis function neuroarchitecture.

The first and the fourth hidden layers, in contrast to the previously considered neuro-fuzzy systems, contain adaptive multidimensional wavelet activation-membership functions that were described above. There are $h_\psi n$ multidimensional wavelets $\psi_{ji}(x(k)) = \psi_{ij}(x(k), c_{ji}^{\psi}, R_{ji}^{-1}(k), \alpha_{ji}^{\psi})$ in the first hidden layer, and $h_\varphi n$ multidimensional wavelets $\varphi_{jm}(x(k)) = \varphi_{im}(x(k), c_{jm}^{\varphi}, Q_{jm}^{-1}(k), \alpha_{jm}^{\varphi})$ whose parameters are adjusted during learning of multilayered wavelet-neuro fuzzy system in the fourth hidden layer.

In order to describe the proposed multidimensional wavelet-neuro-fuzzy system, let us introduce notation for wavelet activation-membership functions:

- in the first layer:

$$\psi_{ji}(x(k)) = \left(1 - \alpha_{ji}^{\psi}(k)\tau_{ji}^{\psi 2}(x(k))\right) \exp\left(-\tau_{ji}^{\psi 2}(x(k))/2\right), \tag{97}$$

- in the fourth layer:

$$\varphi_{jm}(x(k)) = \left(1 - \alpha_{jm}^{\varphi}(k)\tau_{jm}^{\varphi\,2}(x(k))\right) \exp\left(-\tau_{jm}^{\varphi\,2}(x(k))/2\right) \tag{98}$$

where $\tau^{\psi}_{ji} = (x(k)-c^{\psi}_{ji})^T R^{-1}_{ji}(k)(x(k)-c^{\psi}_{ji})$; $\tau^{\varphi}_{ji} = (x(k)-c^{\varphi}_{ji})^T R^{-1}_{ji}(k)(x(k)-c^{\varphi}_{ji})$.

Similar to the previous system, the second hidden layer performs operation that is similar to calculation of T-norm (64), and after that, normalization of form (65) takes place in the third hidden layer, ensuring condition (66) satisfaction (in this case $j=1,2,\ldots,h_{\psi}$).

The fourth hidden layer that implements consequent of the system is based on adaptive W-neurons and is determined by (86). Then values are calculated similar to (87) in the fourth layer, and in the fifth output layer, the system output signal is formed (88), (89).

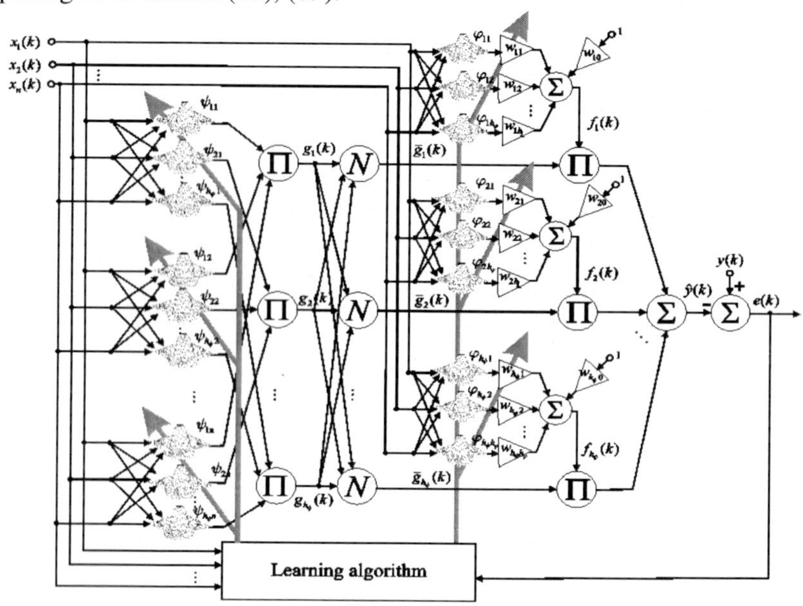

Figure 19. Architecture of hybrid adaptive wavelet-neuro-fuzzy system based on W-neurons with multidimensional adaptive wavelet activation-membership functions in hidden layer.

In order to adjust parameters of the first hidden layer of multidimensional wavelet-neuro-fuzzy system, we use modified method of error back propagation. By performing a set of transformations, we can obtain learning procedure of the first hidden layer with high convergence speed. In order to provide the learning procedure with filtering ability, we introduce additional procedure of regularization parameter adjustment that leads to learning method of parameters c^{ψ}_{ji} and α^{ψ}_{ji} in the form

$$\begin{cases} \Psi(k+1) = \Psi(k) + \lambda_{\Psi}\left(\dfrac{J_{\Psi}(k+1)e(k+1)}{\eta_{\Psi}(k+1)}\right), \\ \eta_{\Psi}(k+1) = \beta\eta_{\Psi}(k) + \| J_{\Psi}(k+1) \|^2 \end{cases} \tag{99}$$

where $J_{\Psi}(k) = \left(\dfrac{\partial y(k)}{\partial c_{11}^{\psi}}, \dfrac{\partial y(k)}{\partial \alpha_{11}^{\psi}}, \ldots, \dfrac{\partial y(k)}{\partial c_{h_{\psi}n}^{\psi}}, \dfrac{\partial y(k)}{\partial \alpha_{h_{\psi}n}^{\psi}}\right)^T$;

$$\begin{cases} \dfrac{\partial y(k)}{\partial c_{ji}^{\psi}} = -\dfrac{2f_j(x(k))\overline{g}_j(k)(1-\overline{g}_j(k))R_{ji}^{-1}(k)(x(k)-c_{ji}^{\psi}(k))}{\psi_{ji}(\tau_{ji}^{\psi}(k))} \cdot \\ \cdot \dfrac{\partial \psi_{ji}(\tau_{ji}^{\psi}(k))}{\partial \tau_{ji}^{\psi}(k)}, \\ \dfrac{\partial y(k)}{\partial \alpha_{ji}^{\psi}} = \dfrac{f_j(x(k))\overline{g}_j(k)(1-\overline{g}_j(k))}{\psi_{ji}(\tau_{ji}^{\psi}(k))} \cdot \dfrac{\partial \psi_{ji}(\tau_{ji}^{\psi}(k))}{\partial \alpha_{ji}^{\psi}(k)}. \end{cases} \tag{100}$$

For the matrix of receptive fields R_{ji}^{-1} the procedure in the vector-matrix form is used

$$\begin{cases} H(k+1) = H(k) + \lambda_H\left(\dfrac{J_H(k)e(k)}{\eta_H(k)}\right), \\ \eta_H(k+1) = \beta\eta_H(k) + Tr(J_H^T(k+1)J_H(k+1)) \end{cases} \tag{101}$$

where $J_H(k) = \left(\left\{\dfrac{\partial y(k)}{\partial R_{11}^{-1}}\right\}, \ldots, \left\{\dfrac{\partial y(k)}{\partial R_{h_{\psi}n}^{-1}}\right\}\right)^T$;

$$\left\{\frac{\partial y(k)}{\partial R_{ji}^{-1}}\right\} = \frac{f_j(x(k))\overline{g}_j(k)(1-\overline{g}_j(k))(x(k)-c_{ji}^{\psi}(k))}{\psi_{ji}(\tau_{ji}^{\psi}(k))} \cdot \frac{\partial \psi_{ji}(\tau_{ji}^{\psi}(k))}{\partial \tau_{ji}^{\psi}(k)}. \tag{102}$$

In this cases the learning algorithm for the fourth layer is identical to learning algorithm of forth layer in one-dimensional wavelet-neuro-fuzzy-network based on W-neuron and described by the expressions (95), (96).

Hybrid Evolving Wavelet-Neuro-Fuzzy-Systems with Tuned Architectures

Acute problem in the dynamical data mining is problem of architecture network choice. And in the unsuccessful choice case it leads to loss of quality problem solving as well as to an increase in training time due to redundancy of the parameters that must be tuned. On the other hand, also there is the problem of multi-dimensional data processing, whereby the rapidly increasing of system adjustable parameters. So, actual problem is development of new architectures and learning algorithms based on hybrid evolving adaptive wavelet-neuro-fuzzy-systems, that allows tuning of system architecture in the solving process of dynamical data mining, and also allows to selection input variable for the choice of the most informative. Hybridization of inductive modelling methods based on GMDH, evolving approach, and cascaded neural networks with previously developed neurons allow solving of such type problems and dynamical data mining on the new quality level.

Hybrid Multilayer GMDH-Wavelet-Neural Network with Different Type of Wavelet-Neuro-Fuzzy Nodes

In order to improve the solution quality of non-stationary signal processing tasks appropriate to introduce the GMDH-neural network with nodes based on wavelet-neuron, multidimensional W-neuron, wavelet-neuro-fuzzy systems [30].

Let is introduce the evolving multilayered GMDH-neural network, which architecture is shown in Figure 20. In this case, it is possible extension of the inputs in the network nodes due to using proposed hybrid neurons.

To the zero (receptive) network layer $(n\times 1)$-dimensional vector of input signals $x=(x_1,x_2,...,x_n)^{\mathrm{T}}$ is fed. This signal then is fed to the first hidden layer containing $n_1=C_n^3$ compartmental neurons, on the outputs of which the signals $\hat{y}_l^{[1]}$, $l=1,2,\ldots,1/6n(n-1)(n-2)$ appear. These signals are fed to the selection block of the first hidden layer $SB^{[1]}$ that selects from the set $\hat{y}_l^{[1]}$ the best from the standpoint of variance $\sigma^2_{\hat{y}_l^{[1]}}$ $n_1^*<n_1$ signals. From selected signals $n_2=C_{n_1^*}^3$ all possible combinations $\hat{y}_i^{[1]}$, $\hat{y}_j^{[1]}$, $\hat{y}_g^{[1]}$ are formed. After

what these combinations are fed to the second hidden layer, formed by $W-N^{[2]}$ neurons. From the output signals of the layer $\hat{y}_l^{[2]}$ selection block $SB^{[2]}$ takes only those that outperform the best signal of first hidden layer $\hat{y}_l^{[1]*}$ by accuracy. The third hidden layer forms signals that outperform the best signal $\hat{y}_l^{[2]*}$, etc. Network evolution process goes until selection block $SB^{[\nu-1]}$ will form on its output only three signals $\hat{y}_1^{[\nu-1]}$, $\hat{y}_2^{[\nu-1]}$ and $\hat{y}_3^{[\nu-1]}$. Exactly these three signals are fed to the output neuron $W-N^{[\nu]}$ that computes network output signal $\hat{y}_l^{[\nu]*}$ and in so doing the condition $\sigma^2_{\hat{y}_l^{[\nu]}} < \sigma^2_{\hat{y}_l^{[\nu-1]*}} < \ldots < \sigma^2_{\hat{y}_l^{[1]*}}$ executes automatically.

Advantages of proposed approach are possibility of inputs selection, small samples processing and other.

Simulation of proposed hybrid multilayer GMDH-neural network based on W-neurons with robust learning algorithm was performed based on non-stationary signal, which is noised by intensive outliers. The signal was obtained by equation of nonlinear dynamical plant of Narendra-Parthasarathy [48], whose output signal was disturbed by random outliers with Cauchy distribution (heavy tails distribution) in the form

$$F_X^{-1}(x) = x_0 + \gamma \tan\left[\pi\left(x - \frac{1}{2}\right)\right], \tag{103}$$

and nonlinear dynamic plant was generated by equation in the form

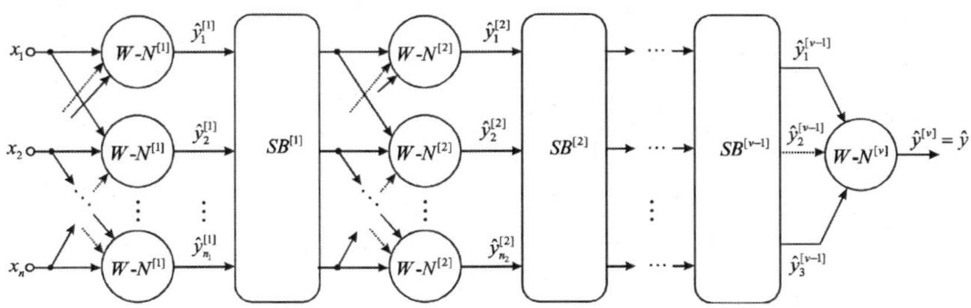

Figure 20. Evolving multilayer GMDH-neural network architecture.

$$y(k+1) = 0.3y(k) + 0.6y(k-1) + f(u(k))\,. \tag{104}$$

The values $x(k-3), x(k-2), x(k-1), x(k)$ were used for prediction of value $x(k+1)$. So initial value of the input number was taken as $n=4$, and first layer nodes number of hybrid GMDH-neural network based on W-neurons was taken as $C_4^2=6$. Initial values of learning algorithm parameters were taken as $\delta_w=\delta_c=\delta_Q=\delta_\alpha=0.5$, $\beta_w=\beta_c=\beta_Q=\beta_\alpha=0.99$, $\gamma_w=\gamma_c=\gamma_Q=\gamma_\alpha=0.99$.

The learning sample consists of 2000 points, and next 1000 points were using as testing sample. The testing sample consists of $f(u(k))=0.6\sin u(k)+0.3\sin(3u(k))+0.1\sin(5u(k))$ and $u(k)=sin(2\pi k/250)$ for $k=2001\ldots2500$ and $f(u(k))=u^3(k)+0.3u^2(k)+0.4u(k)$ and $u(k)=sin(2\pi k/250)+sin(2\pi k/25)$ for $k=2501\ldots3000$. Initial values of synaptic weights were taken randomly in the interval [-0.1; 0.1].

Figure 21,a shows the results of noised nonstationary dynamical signal forecasting, and Figure 21,b shows fragment of learning process. Here it can see that outliers with large amplitude located at the begin of sample did not influence to the learning process.

The best prediction result of the proposed system with robust learning algorithm are provided. In the case when only synaptic weights are tuned by robust learning algorithm, prediction error is increased.

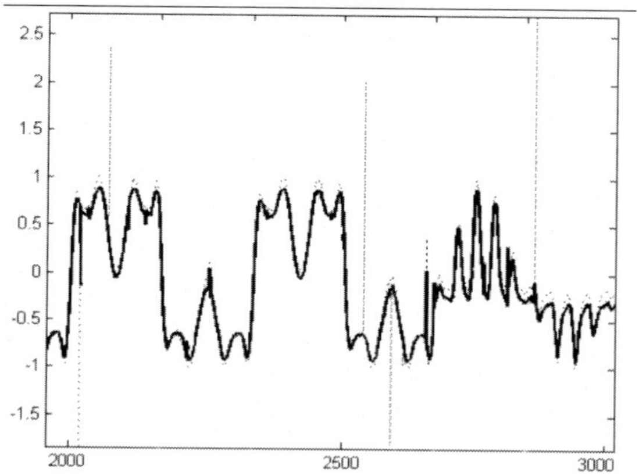

(a)

Figure 21. (Continued).

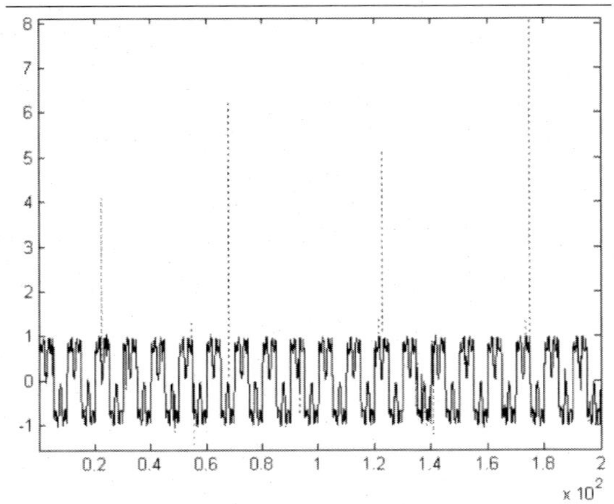

(b)

Figure 21. Prediction result of non-linear non-stationary time series.

When training system is provided by gradient method the first outlier in the begin of sample strongly influences to the learning process and leads to a big prediction error.

Table 1. Comparative analysis of prediction non-linear non-stationary signal results

Neural network/Learning algorithm	Number of layers	Number of inputs into nodes	RMSE
Hybrid multilayer GMDH-neural network based on W-neurons/Proposed robust learning algorithm (tuning all-parameters of nodes)	3	3	0.041
Hybrid multilayer GMDH-neural network based on W-neurons/Proposed robust learning algorithm (tuning all-parameters of nodes)	3	2	0.056
Hybrid multilayer GMDH-neural network based on W-neurons/Proposed robust learning algorithm (tuning only synaptic weights)	3	2	0.062
Hybrid multilayer GMDH-neural network based on W-neurons/Gradient learning algorithm	4	2	0.087
Hybrid multilayer GMDH-neural network based on W-neurons/LSM	4	2	∞
GMDH-neural network/Gradient learning algorithm	4	2	1.45

When training system is provided by least squares method the first outlier leads to so-called “burst parameters” of covariance matrix and as a result - the inability to predict the signal which is noised by abnormal outliers.

Table 1 shows comparative analysis of prediction non-linear non-stationary signal based on different approaches.

Thus, it is seen that the proposed robust learning algorithm allows the signals processing under conditions of significant contamination abnormal outliers.

Efficiency of hybrid multilayer GMDH-neural network based on wavelet neurons was examined based on solving forecasting problem of real ecological time series. This time sequence describes monthly pressure above the sea level from 1882 to 1998 (Darwin sea level pressure). This time series is a key indicator of climate change, as well as important in the study of the effect of the El Niño or Southern Oscillation index.

Inputs number of hybrid GMDH-neural network based wavelet neurons were taken as $n_{GMDH} = 6$, that for input vector in the form $x(k-5), x(k-4), x(k-3), x(k-2), x(k-1), x(k)$ for the prediction value $x(k+1)$. Wavelet neuron was training using proposed learning algorithm during 900 iterations (900 points of training sample for $k = 1 \ldots 900$). Initial parameters values of learning algorithm were taken $\eta_c = \eta_Q = \eta_\alpha = 10000$, and shape parameter value of adaptive wavelet membership-activation function was taken as $\alpha = 0.5$. After 900 iterations the training process was stopped, and the next 500 points for $k = 901 \ldots 1400$ we have used as the testing data set to compute forecast. Initial values of synaptic weights were taken equal to 0. As the quality criterion of forecasting root mean square error (MSE) was used.

Figure 22 shows the results of time series forecasting. The two curves, representing the actual (dot line) and forecasting (solid line) values, are almost indistinguishable.

Table 2 shows comparative analysis of forecasting time series based on different approaches.

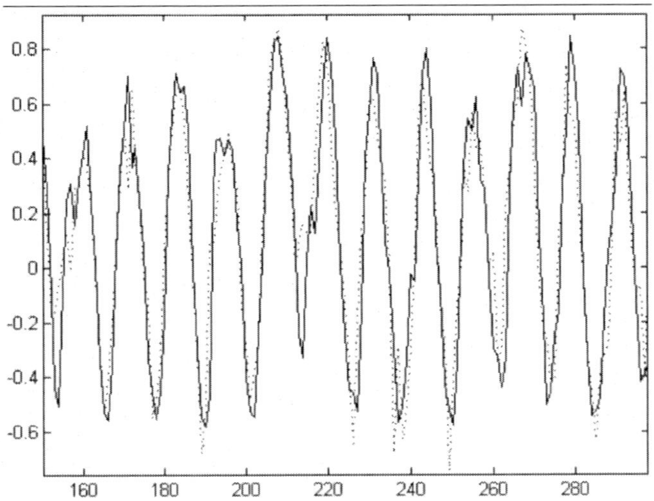

Figure 22. Results of time series forecasting.

Table 2. Comparative analysis of forecasting time series results

Neural network/Learning algorithm	Number of layers	Number of inputs into nodes	MSE
Hybrid multilayer GMDH-neural network based on wavelet neurons/Proposed learning algorithm (tuning all-parameters of nodes)	2	3	0.0035
Hybrid multilayer GMDH-neural network based on wavelet neurons/Proposed learning algorithm (tuning all-parameters of nodes)	3	2	0.0098
Hybrid multilayer GMDH-neural network based on wavelet neurons/Proposed learning algorithm (tuning only synaptic weights)	3	2	0.0273
Hybrid multilayer GMDH-neural network based on wavelet neurons/RLSM	3	2	0.0998
Hybrid multilayer GMDH-neural network based on wavelet neurons/Gradient learning algorithm	3	2	0.1018

Thus as it can be seen from experimental results the proposed approach having the best quality of prediction in comparison with conventional GMDH-neural network.

Cascade Wavelet Neural Network and its Learning

The main disadvantage of conventional cascade networks is impossibility of their learning process in on-line mode due to the type of used artificial neurons – elementary Rosenblatt perceptrons [49]. As is known in such neurons the sigmoidal or hyperbolic tangent functions are used as activation functions and as a result of the output signal of each neuron depends nonlinearly from the synaptic weights. So learning process should be performed using the delta-rule and its modifications, which are gradient optimization algorithms. Obviously, it is difficult to talk about optimizing of the learning rate and learning process in on-line mode in this case.

In the connection with that it seems appropriate to synthesize the hybrid cascade architecture, where the cascades use neurons, in which the output signal linearly depends of the synaptic weights that permits to optimize learning speed and reduce the size of the training set.

As the nodes of such cascade-correlation network the wavelet-neurons are proposed. The expression (11) describes output of wavelet-neuron. As the learning algorithm, we used procedure in the form

$$\begin{cases} w_i(k+1) = w_i(k) + \dfrac{e(k+1)\varphi_i(x_i(k+1))}{r_i^w(k+1)}, \\ r_i^w(k+1) = \beta r_i^w(k) + \| \varphi_i^w(k+1) \|^2 \end{cases} \quad (105)$$

where $\varphi_i(x_i(k)) = (\varphi_{1i}(x_i(k)), \ldots, \varphi_{h_i i}(x_i)(k))^T$ is $(h_i \times 1)$ - vector of wavelet-activation functions, $w_i(k) = (w_{1i}(k), \ldots, w_{h_i i})^T$ is $(h_i \times 1)$ - vector of synaptic weight of i -th wavelet-synapse.

Replacing neurons in the nodes of the cascade network by the elements, whose output signals are linearly dependent of the synaptic weight we can escape disadvantages and even get some useful properties due to the choice of artificial neuron type.

Replacing Rosenblatt perceptrons in nodes of cascade correlation neural networks which were proposed by Fahlman and Lebier on the wavelet-neurons we can to introduce hybrid wavelet cascade architecture shown in Figure 23 [50].

Such cascade wavelet-neural network realizes mapping of the following form:

- wavelet-neuron of first cascade

$$\hat{y}^{[1]} = \sum_{i=1}^{n}\sum_{j=1}^{h} w_{ji}^{[1]} \varphi_{ji}(x_i), \tag{106}$$

- wavelet-neuron of second cascade

$$\hat{y}^{[2]} = \sum_{i=1}^{n}\sum_{j=1}^{h} w_{ji}^{[2]} \varphi_{ji}(x_i) + \sum_{j=1}^{h} w_{j,n+1}^{[2]} \varphi_{j,n+1}(\hat{y}^{[1]}), \tag{107}$$

- wavelet-neuron of third cascade

$$\hat{y}^{[3]} = \sum_{i=1}^{n}\sum_{j=1}^{h} w_{ji}^{[3]} \varphi_{ji}(x_i) + \sum_{j=1}^{h} w_{j,n+1}^{[3]} \varphi_{j,n+1}(\hat{y}^{[1]}) + \sum_{j=1}^{h} w_{j,n+2}^{[3]} \varphi_{j,n+2}(\hat{y}^{[2]}), \tag{108}$$

- wavelet-neuron of m-th cascade

$$\hat{y}^{[m]} = \sum_{i=1}^{n}\sum_{j=1}^{h} w_{ji}^{[m]} \varphi_{ji}(x_i) + \sum_{l=n+1}^{n+m-1}\sum_{j=1}^{h} w_{jl}^{[m]} \varphi_{jl}(\hat{y}^{[l-n]}). \tag{109}$$

The cascade wavelet neural network learning is performed using full training set $\{x(1), y(1); x(2), y(2); \ldots;\ x(k), y(k); x(N), y(N)\}$.

At the beginning a set of wavelet-functions values (2) $\varphi^{[1]}(1), \varphi^{[1]}(2), \ldots,$ $\varphi^{[1]}(N)$ is calculated for each training sample.

Then using direct minimization of the learning criterion

$$E_N^{[1]} = \frac{1}{2}\sum_{k=1}^{N} e_1^2(k) = \frac{1}{2}\sum_{k=1}^{N}(y(k) - \hat{y}_1(k))^2, \tag{110}$$

the vector of synaptic weights can be computed as

$$w^{[1]}(N) = \left(\sum_{k=1}^{N}\varphi^{[1]}(k)\varphi^{[1]T}(k)\right)^{+} \sum_{k=1}^{N}\varphi^{[1]}(k)y(k) = P^{[1]}(N)\sum_{k=1}^{N}\varphi^{[1]}(k)y(k) \tag{111}$$

where $\bullet^{+}$ is symbol of Moore-Penrose pseudoinverse.

If dimension of this vector is sufficiently large it is suitable to use procedure based on recursive least squares method with sequential training samples processing:

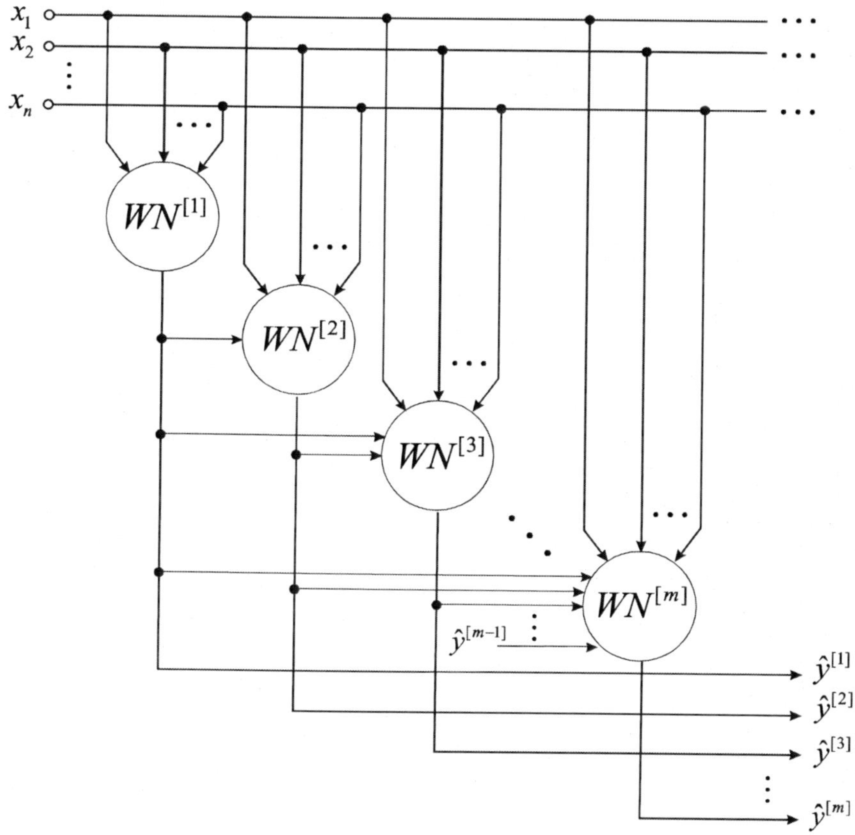

Figure 23. Hybrid cascade wavelet neural network.

$$\begin{cases} w^{[1]}(k+1) = w^{[1]}(k) + \dfrac{P^{[1]}(k)\ \ y(k+1) - w^{[1]T}(k)\varphi^{[1]}(k+1)}{1+\varphi^{[1]T}(k+1)P^{[1]}(k)\varphi^{[1]}(k+1)}\varphi^{[1]}(k+1), \\ P^{[1]}(k+1) = P^{[1]}(k) - \dfrac{P^{[1]}(k)\varphi^{[1]}(k+1)\varphi^{[1]T}(k+1)P^{[1]}(k)}{1+\varphi^{[1]T}(k+1)P^{[1]}(k)\varphi^{[1]}(k+1)}, \quad P^{[1]} = \theta\mathbf{I} \end{cases} \tag{112}$$

where θ – is sufficiently large positive number which is defined empirically, $\mathbf{I}$ is unity matrix of appropriate dimensionality.

It is necessary to notice that using procedures (111), (112) for adjusting weight coefficients essentially reduces learning time in comparison with gradient algorithms underlying delta-rule [51].

After first cascade learning completion, synaptic weights of the neuron $WN^{[1]}$ become 'frozen' and second cascade of network consisting from a single neuron $WN^{[2]}$ is generated. It has one additional input for the output signal of the first cascade. Then procedures (110), (111) again are applied for adjusting of weight coefficients vector $w^{[2]}$, with dimensionality $(h+1)(n+1)\times 1$.

The neural network growing process (increasing cascades number) continues until we obtain required precision of the solved problem's solution, and for the adjusting weight coefficients of the last m-th cascade following expression are used:

$$w^{[m]}(N)=\left(\sum_{k=1}^{N}\varphi^{[m]}(k)\varphi^{[m]T}(k)\right)^{+}\sum_{k=1}^{N}\varphi^{[m]}(k)y(k)=P^{[m]}(N)\sum_{k=1}^{N}\varphi^{[m]}(k)y(k) \quad (113)$$

in batch mode,

$$\begin{cases} w^{[m]}(k+1)=w^{[m]}(k)+\dfrac{P^{[m]}(k)\ y(k+1)-w^{[m]T}(k)\varphi^{[m]}(k+1)}{1+\varphi^{[m]T}(k+1)P^{[m]}(k)\varphi^{[m]}(k+1)}\varphi^{[m]}(k+1), \\ P^{[m]}(k+1)=P^{[m]}(k)-\dfrac{P^{[m]}(k)\varphi^{[m]}(k+1)\varphi^{[m]T}(k+1)P^{[m]}(k)}{1+\varphi^{[m]T}(k+1)P^{[m]}(k)\varphi^{[m]}(k+1)},\ P^{[m]}=\theta\mathbf{I} \end{cases} \quad (114)$$

or

$$\begin{cases} w^{[m]}(k+1)=w^{[m]}(k)+\dfrac{e(k+1)\varphi^{[m]}(k+1)}{\eta^{[m]}(k+1)}, \\ \eta^{[m]}(k+1)=\beta\eta^{[m]}(k)+\|\varphi^{[m]}(k+1)\|^{2},\quad 0\le\beta\le 1 \end{cases} \quad (115)$$

in on-line mode of information processing.

The main disadvantage of conventional cascade-correlation network is connected with the batch mode learning, when all training set should be given a-priori. Cascade wavelet neural network can be trained in on-line mode, because of algorithm (114) possess maximal possible squared rate of convergence.

In this case at the first step architecture consisting of m cascades is generated. Each cascade trains using proper algorithm. Since outputs of the previous wavelet-neurons become additional inputs for the m-th cascade, algorithm realizes recurrent method of the prediction error, well known in the theory of adaptive identification. Changing cascades number during learning process also can be easily performed.

Evolving Cascade GMDH-Wavelet-Neural Network

Computational unhandiness of multilayer GMDH-NN forces to look for alternative variant in the capacity of which evolving cascade GMDH-NN [52] can be used. Its architecture is shown in Figure 24.

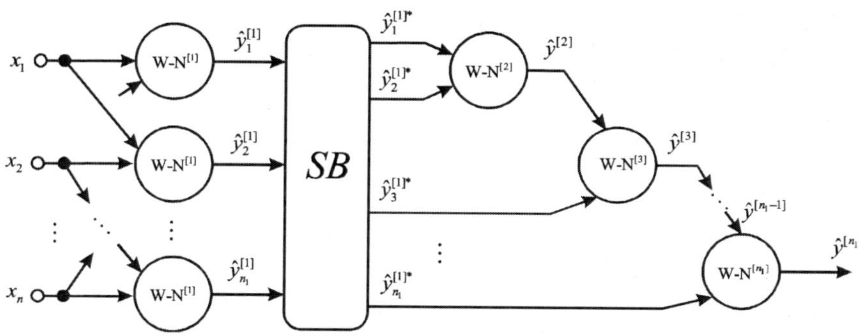

Figure 24. Evolving cascade GMDH-neural network.

The first hidden layer of this network is analogous to the first layer of network presented on Figure 20 with the only difference that selection block SB performs ranking of all the signals $\hat{y}_l^{[1]}$ so, that $\sigma^2_{\hat{y}_1^{[1]*}} < \sigma^2_{\hat{y}_2^{[1]*}} < \ldots < \sigma^2_{\hat{y}_{n_1}^{[1]*}}$.

In this case, nodes with two inputs are used.

First layer (cascade) outputs $\hat{y}_1^{[1]*}$ and $\hat{y}_2^{[1]*}$ are fed to the only neuron of the second cascade $W-N^{[2]}$ forming signal $\hat{y}^{[2]}$ that further in the third cascade is united with selection block output $\hat{y}_3^{[1]*}$. The process of cascades increasing is continued until required accuracy is obtained. The overall neurons number of such a network is defined by the value $2n_1 - 1$.

In case, if the achieved accuracy is not satisfactory, it can be improved by tuning not only the synaptic weights, but also centers, width and shape parameters of hybrid neuron.

Naturally, after tuning of centers and width parameters, it is necessary to recalculate the synaptic weights. If, for some reason, this configuration is not desired, we can try to improve the approximation properties of hybrid neurons, placing them centers based on more effective clustering methods.

Simulation of evolving cascaded GMDH-neural network based on W-neurons was performed in the process of identification of nonlinear signal, which is described by equation in the form [44]

$$y(k+1) = \frac{y(k)}{1 + y^2(k)} + u^3(k) \tag{116}$$

where $u(k) = sin(2\pi k / 25) + sin(2\pi k / 10)$ is control signal.

The inputs number of evolving cascaded GMDH-neural network were taken as $n_{GMDH} = 4$, which correspond to the input vector $x(k-3), x(k-2), x(k-1), x(k)$ for the value $x(k+1)$.

Each W-neuron contains 7 adaptive wavelet membership-activation functions. W-neuron was trained in batch mode based on proposed procedures for 1500 iterations (1500 training samples for $k = 1\ldots1500$). Initial values of the learning algorithm were taken as $\eta_c = \eta_Q = \eta_\alpha = 10000$, and shape parameters of adaptive wavelet membership-activation functions were taken as $\alpha = 1$. After 1500 iterations the training process was stopped, and the next 500 points for $(k = 1501\ldots2000)$ we have used as the testing data set to compute forecast. Initial values of synaptic weights were taken equal to 0. As the quality criterion of forecasting root mean square error (MSE) was used.

Figure 25 shows the results of signal identification. The two curves, representing the actual (dot line) and forecasting (solid line) values, are almost indistinguishable. Table 3 shows the comparative analysis of nonlinear non-stationary plant identification based on different approaches.

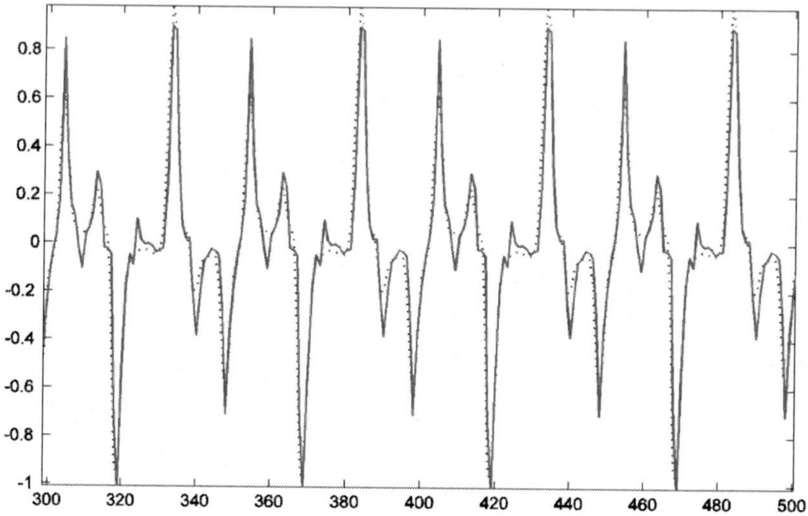

Figure 25. Results of non-linear non-stationary system identification.

Table 3. Comparative analysis of time series identification results

Neural network	*MSE*
Evolving cascaded GMDH neural network based on W-neurons	0.0009
Evolving cascaded GMDH neural network based on R-neurons with Gaussian functions	0.0023
Evolving cascaded GMDH neural network based on R-neurons with Epanechnikov functions	0.0015
Hybrid multilayer GMDH neural network based on W-нейронов	0.0058
Hybrid multilayer GMDH neural network based on R-neurons with Gaussian functions	0.0103
Hybrid multilayer GMDH neural network based on R-neurons with Epanechnikov functions	0.0098
Multilayer GMDH-neural network with polynomial functions	0.0201

Thus as it can be seen from experimental results the proposed approach having the best quality of prediction in comparison with considered approaches due to tuning of all-parameters of adaptive wavelet membership-activation function of each W-neuron.

REFERENCES

[1] Raghavan, V. and Hafez, A. (2000). Dynamic Data Mining. *J. of the American Society for Information Science*, *LNAI*, *1821*, 220-229.

[2] Lughofer, E. (2011). Evolving Fuzzy Systems: Methodologies, Advanced Concepts and Applications. Berlin Heidelberg: Springer.

[3] Angelov, P., Filev, D. and Kasabov, N. (2010). Evolving Intelligent Systems: Methodology and Applications. N.Y.: John Willey and Sons.

[4] Ivakhnenko, A. G., Wuensch, D. and Ivakhnenko, G. A. (1999). Inductive sorting-out GMDH algorithms with polynomial complexity for active neurons of neural network. *Neural Networks*, *2*, 1169-1173.

[5] Ivakhnenko, A. G. (1970). Heuristic self-organization in problems of engineering cybernetics. *Automatica*, *6*(2), 207-219.

[6] Ivakhnenko, A. G. (1971). Polynomial theory of complex systems. *IEEE Trans. on Systems*, *Man*, *Cybernetics*, *1*(4), 364-378.

[7] Ivakhnenko, A. G. (1995). Self-organization of neuro net with active neurons for effects of nuclear test explosions forecasting. *System Analysis Modeling Simulation*, *20*, 107-116.

[8] Bulgakova, O. and Samoylenko, O. (2007). Comparing NN and GMDH methods for prediction of socio-economic processes. *Proc. of the II International Workshop on Inductive Modelling*. Prague: Czech Technical University, 217-220.

[9] Kondo, T. (1998). GMDH neural network algorithm using the heuristic self-organization method and its application to the pattern identification problem. *Proc. of SICE Annual Conference Japan*, *Tokyo*, 1143-1148.

[10] Kondo, T. and Ueno, J. (2010). Nonlinear system identification by feedback GMDH-type neural network with architecture self-selecting function. *Proc. IEEE International Symposium on Intelligent Control*, 1521-1526.

[11] Kondo, T. and Pandya, A. S. (2003). Structural identification of the multi-layered neural networks by using revised GMDH-type neural network algorithm with a feedback loop. *Proc. of the SICE Annual Conference, Japan, Tokyo*, 2806-2811.

[12] Yamakawa, T., Uchino, E., Miki, T. and Kusanagi H. (1992). A neo-fuzzy neuron and its application to system identification and prediction of the system behavior. *Proc. 2nd Int. Conf. on Fuzzy Logic and Neural Networks, Iizuka, Japan*, 477-483.

[13] Miki, I. and Yamakawa, I. (1999) Analog implementation of neo-fuzzy neuron and its on-board learning. Computational Intelligence and Applications. Piraeus: WSES Press., 144-149.

[14] Bodyanskiy, Ye., Kokshenev, I. and Kolodyazhniy, V. An adaptive learning algorithm for a neo-fuzzy neuron. *Proc. 3rd Int. Conf. of European Union Soc. for Fuzzy Logic and Technology (EUSFLAT 2003)*, Zittau, Germany, 2003, 375-379.

[15] Tsoukalas, L. H. and Uhrig, R. E. (1997). Fuzzy and Neural Approaches in Engineering. N.Y.: John Willey and Sons, Inc.

[16] Kaczmarz, S. (1993). Approximate solution of systems of linear equations. *Int. J. Control*, *53*, 1269-1271.

[17] Widrow, B. and Hoff Jr, M. E. Adaptive switching circuits. (1960). *IRE Western Electric Show and Connection Record*, Part 4, 96-104.

[18] Bodyanskiy, Ye., Lamonova, N., Pliss, I. and Vynokurova, O. (2005). An adaptive learning algorithm for a wavelet neural network. *Expert Systems*, *22*(5), 235-240.

[19] Lekutai, G. and van Landingham, H. F. (1997). Self-tuning control of nonlinear systems using neural network adaptive frame wavelets. *Proc. IEEE Int. Conf. on Systems, Man and Cybernetics, Piscataway*, N.J., *2*, 1017-1022.

[20] Bodyanskiy, Ye., Vynokurova, O. and Yegorova, E. (2008). Radial-basis-fuzzy-wavelet-neural network with adaptive activation-membership function. *Int. J. on Artificial Intelligence and Machine Learning*, *8*(II), 9-15.

[21] Bodyanskiy, Ye. and Vynokurova, O. (2009). Compartmental adaptive wavelon and its learning algorithm. *Control Systems and Computers*, *1*(219), 47-53 (In Russian).

[22] Mitaim, S. and Kosko, B. (1996). What is the best shape for a fuzzy set in function approximation? *Proc. 5th IEEE Int. Conf on Fuzzy Systems "Fuzz-96,"* *2*, 1237-1213.

[23] Mitaim, S. and Kosko, B. (1997). Adaptive joint fuzzy sets for function approximation. *Proc. Int. Conf. on Neural Networks "ICNN-97,"* 537-542.

[24] Shepherd, A. J. (1997). *Second-Order Methods for Neural Networks*. London: Springer-Verlag.

[25] Bodyanskiy, Ye., Kolodyazhniy, V. and Stephan, A. (2001). An adaptive learning algorithm for a neuro-fuzzy network. *Computational Intelligence and Applications*, 68-75.

[26] Goodwin, G. C., Ramadge, P. J. and Caines, P. E. (1981). A globally convergent adaptive predictor. *Automatica*, *17*(1), 135-140.

[27] Park, J. and Sandberg, I. W. (1991). Universal approximation using radial-basis-function networks. *Neural Computation*, *3*, 246-257.

[28] Sunil, E. V. T. and Yung, C. Sh. (1994). Radial basis function neural network for approximation and estimation of nonlinear stochastic dynamic systems. *IEEE Trans. on Neural Networks*, *5*, 594-603.

[29] Bishop, C. M. (1995). *Neural Networks for Pattern Recognition.* Oxford: Clarendon Press.

[30] Bodyanskiy, Ye., Pliss, I. and Vynokurova, O. (2009). Hybrid GMDH-neural network of computational intelligence. Proc. 3rd International Workshop on Inductive Modelling, Poland, Krynica, 100-107.

[31] Bodyanskiy, Ye., Pliss, I. and Teslenko, N. (2010). GMDH-neural network based on compartmental R-neurons with activation function kind of multidimensional Epanechnikov kernels. Proc. of 5 Int. conf. Decision-making theory. Uzhgorod, UzNU, 27-28 (In Russian).

[32] Itakura, F. (1975). Maximum prediction residual principle applied to speech recognition. *IEEE Trans. on Acoustics, Speech, and Signal Processing*, *23*, 67-72.

[33] Jang, J. S. R. and Sun, C. T. (1993). Functional equivalence between radial basis function networks and fuzzy inference systems. *IEEE Trans. on Neural Networks*, *4*, 156-159.

[34] Hunt, K. J., Haas, R. and Smith R. M. (1996). Extending the functional equivalence of radial basis function networks and fuzzy inference systems. *IEEE Trans. on Neural Networks*, *7*, 776-781.

[35] Reyneri, L. M. (1999). Unification of neural and wavelet networks and fuzzy systems. *IEEE Trans. on Neural Networks*, *10*, 801-814.

[36] Bodyanskiy, Ye. and Vynokurova, O. (2008). Hybrid radial-basis neuro-fuzzy wavelon in the non-stationary sequences forecasting problems. Proc. of 2nd Int. Conf. on Inductive Modelling, Kyiv, 144-147.

[37] Bodyanskiy, Ye. and Vynokurova, O. (2011). Hybrid type-2 wavelet-neuro-fuzzy network for businesses process prediction. *Business Informatics*, *21*, 9-21.

[38] Ljung, L. (1999). System Identification: Theory for the User. N.J.: PTR Prentice Hall, Upper Saddle River.

[39] Rajbman, N. S. and Chadeev, V. M. (1966). Adaptive models in control systems. M.: Sov. radio.

[40] Bodyanskiy, Ye., Vynokurova, O. and Pavlov, O. (2008). Outliers resistant learning algorithm for radial-basis-fuzzy-wavelet-neural

network in stomach acute injury diagnosis tasks. *Information Science and Computing*, *2*, 55-62.

[41] Bodyanskiy, Ye., Pavlov, O. and Vynokurova, O. (2009). Adaptive compartmental wavelon with robust learning algorithm. *Int. J. on Information Technologies and Knowledge*, *3*, 24-36.

[42] Wang, L. X. (1994). Adaptive Fuzzy Systems and Control: Design and Stability Analysis. New Jersey: Prentice Hall.

[43] Bodyanskiy, Ye., Pliss, I. and Vynokurova, O. (2008). Adaptive wavelet-neuro-fuzzy network in the forecasting and emulation tasks. *Int. J. on Information Theory and Applications*, *15*(1), 47-55.

[44] Bodyanskiy, Ye., Pliss, I. and Vynokurova, O. (2010). Hybrid wavelet-neuro-fuzzy system using adaptive W-neurons. *Wissenschaftliche Berichte, FH Zittau/Goerlitz*, *106* (N.2454-2490), 301-308.

[45] Bodyanskiy, Ye. and Vynokurova, O. (2013). Hybrid adaptive wavelet-neuro-fuzzy system for chaotic time series identification. *Information Science*, *220*, 170-179.

[46] Abiyev, R. H. and Kaynak, O. (2008). Identification and control of dynamic plant using fuzzy wavelet neural networks. *Proc. of IEEE Int. Symposium on Intelligent Control*, USA: San Antonio, 1295-1301.

[47] Abiyev, R. H. and Kaynak, O. (2008). Fuzzy wavelet neural networks for identification and control of dynamic plants - A novel structure and a comparative study. *IEEE Trans. on Industrial Electronics*, *55*(8), 3133-3140.

[48] Narendra, K. S. and Parthasarathy, K. (1990). Identification and control of dynamical systems using neural networks. *IEEE Trans. on Neural Networks*, *1*, 4-26.

[49] Rosenblatt, F. (1961). Principles of Neurodynamics. Washington D.C.: Spartan Press.

[50] Bodyanskiy, Ye., Kharchenko, O. and Vynokurova, O. (2011). Hybrid cascade neural network based on wavelet-neuron. *Int. J. Information Theories and Application*, *18*(4), 335-343.

[51] Haykin, S. (1999). *Neural Networks. A Comprehensive Foundation*. Upper Saddle River, N.J.: Prentice Hall, Inc.

[52] Bodyanskiy, Ye., Teslenko, N. and Vynokurova, O. (2011). Cascade GMDH-wavelet-neuro-fuzzy network. Proc. of Int. Workshop Inductive Modelling, Kyiv, 22-30.

Biographical Sketches

Yevgeniy Bodyanskiy

Affiliation: Kharkiv National University of Radio Electronics

Education: In 1971 he graduated with honour from Kharkiv National University of Radio Electronics. In 1980 he defended the Ph.D. thesis. In 1984 he received an academic title of Senior Researcher. In 1990 he defended the Doctor Thesis (Dr. habil. sc. ing.). In 1994 he received an academic title of Professor.

Address: 14 Nauky av., Kharkiv, 61166, Ukraine, e-mail: yevgeniy. bodyanskiy@nure.ua.

Research and Professional Experience: Since 1974 he has been working at Kharkiv National University of Radio Electronics. He is a Professor of Artificial Intelligence Department and Head of the Control Systems Research Laboratory at Kharkiv National University of Radio Electronics.

Professional Appointments: hybrid systems of computational intelligence, adaptive, neuro-, wavelet-, neo-fuzzy-, real-time systems, including problems connected with control, identification, forecasting, clustering, diagnostics, fault detection in technical, economical, medical and ecological objects.

Publications: He has more than 640 scientific publications, including 40 inventions and 12 monographs. Publications Last 3 Years:

1. Bodyanskiy Ye., Vynokurova O. Hybrid adaptive wavelet-neuro-fuzzy system for chaotic time series identification//Information Sciences. – 2013. – 220. - P.170-179.
2. Bodyanskiy Ye., Dolotov A., Vynokurova O. Evolving spiking wavelet-neuro-fuzzy self-learning system//Applied Soft Computing. – 2014. – 14. – P. 252-258.
3. Bodyanskiy Ye., Vynokurova E.A., Dolotov A.I. Self-learning cascade spiking neural network for fuzzy clustering based on Group

Method of Data Handling//J. of Automation and Information Sciences. – 2013. – 45. – №3. – P.23-33.

4. Bodyanskiy Ye., Kolchygin B. Adaptive fuzzy clustering with a variable fuzzifier//Cybernetics and System Analysis. – 2013. – 49. - №3. – P.176-181.
5. Bodyanskiy Ye., Tyshchenko O.K., Kopaliani D.S. A hybrid cascade neural network with an optimized pool in each cascade//Soft Computing. A Fusion of Foundations, Methodologies and Applications. – Soft Computing
6. Bodyanskiy Ye., Boiko O.O., Pliss I.P. Adaptive method of hybrid learning for evolving neuro-fuzzy system//Cybernetics and Systems Analysis. – 2015. – Vol. 51. – №. 4. – P. 500-505.
7. Bodyanskiy Ye., Shafronenko A., Volkova V. Adaptive fuzzy probabilistic clustering of incomplete data //Int. J. "Information Models and Analyses." – 2013. – 2. - №2. – P.112-117.
8. Bodyanskiy Ye., Tyshchenko O., Pliss I. Reservoir forecasting neuro-fuzzy network and its learning//Int. J. "Information Theories and Applications." – 2013. – 20. - №3. – P.203-209.
9. Bodyanskiy Ye., Tyshchenko O., Wojcik W. Multivariate non-stationary time series predictor based on an adaptive neuro-fuzzy approach//Elektronika – konstrukcje, technologie, zastosowania. – № 8. – 2013. – P. 10-13.
10. Bodyanskiy Ye., Dolotov A. A spiking neuron model based on the Lambert W-function //Proc. 5th Int. Joint Conf. on Computational Intelligence. – Vilamoura, Algarve, Portugal, 20-22 Sept., 2013. – P. 542-546.
11. Bodyanskiy Ye., Pliss I., Vynokurova O. Flexible neo-fuzzy-neuron and neuro-fuzzy network for monitoring time-series properties//Sci. J. of Riga Technical University: Information Technology and Management Science. – 2013. – 16. – P.47-52.
12. Bodyanskiy Ye., Samitova V., Tyshchenko O. Robust fuzzy data clustering in an ordinal scale based on a similarity measure//Int. J. of Research in Engineering and Science. – 2014. – 2. - №4. – P.21-25.
13. Bodyanskiy Ye., Tyshchenko O., Kopaliani D. A multidimensional cascade neuro-fuzzy system with neuron pool optimization in each cascade//Int. J. Information Technology and Computer Science. – 2014. – 6. - №8. – P. 11-17.

14. Bodyanskiy Ye., Tyshchenko O.K., Kopaliani D.S. An Extended Neo-Fuzzy Neuron and its Adaptive Learning Algorithm//I.J. of Intelligent Systems and Applications (IJISA). - Vol.7, No. 2. - 2015. – P. 21-26.
15. Bodyanskiy Ye., Tyshchenko O.K., Deineko A.O. An Evolving Neuro-Fuzzy System with Online Learning/Self-learning//I.J. of Modern Education and Computer Science (IJMECS). - Vol.7, No. 2. - 2015. – P. 1-7.
16. Bodyanskiy Ye., Kharchenko O., Vynokurova O. Least squares support vector machine based on wavelet-neuron//Sci. J. of Riga Technical University: Information Technology and Management Science. – 17. – 2014. – P. 19-24.
17. Bodyanskiy Ye., Peleshko D., Vynokurova O., Tatarinova Yu. Architecture of Hybrid Generalized Additive Neuro-Fuzzy System in Modelling Technological Process//Proc. XIII-th IEEE Int. Conf. "The Experience of Designing and Application of CAD Systems in Microelectronics." – Lviv-Polyana, Ukraine, 2015. – P. 333-335.
18. Bodyanskiy Ye., Tyshchenko O., Deineko A. Evolving neuro-fuzzy systems with kernel activation functions. Their adaptive learning for Data Mining tasks. – Saarbruecken, Germany: LAP Lambert Academic Publishing. – 2015. – 64 p.
19. Shafronenko A., Bodyanskiy Ye. Robust adaptive fuzzy clustering for data with missing values//Eds. by G. Setlak, K. Markov "Computational Models for Business and Engineering Domains." – Rzeszow-Sofia: ITHEA, 2014. – P. 34-43.
20. Tyshchenko O., Kopaliani D., Bodyanskiy Ye. The least squares support vector machine based on a neo-fuzzy neuron//Eds. by G. Setlak, K. Markov "Computational Models for Business and Engineering Domains." – Rzeszow-Sofia: ITHEA, 2014. – P. 44-51.
21. Vynokurova O., Pliss I., Peleshko D., Bodyanskiy Ye. Multilayer neuro-fuzzy system for solving on-line diagnostics tasks//Eds. by G. Setlak, K. Markov "Computational Models for Business and Engineering Domains." – Rzeszow-Sofia: ITHEA, 2014. – P. 52-59.

Olena Vynokurova

Affiliation: Kharkiv National University of Radio Electronics

Education: In 2002 she graduated with honour from Kharkiv National University of Radio Electronics. In 2005 she defended the Ph.D. thesis. In 2007 she received an academic title of Senior Researcher. In 2012 she defended the Doctor Thesis (Dr. habil. sc. ing.). In 2013 he received an academic title of Professor.

Address: 14 Nauky av., Kharkiv, 61166, Ukraine, e-mail: olena. vynokurova@nure.ua

Research and Professional Experience: Since 2002 he has been working at Kharkiv National University of Radio Electronics. She is Principal Research Scientist of Control Systems Research Laboratory; since 2013 she has been a Professor of the Department of Information Technology Security at Kharkiv National University of Radio Electronics.

Professional Appointments: evolving hybrid systems of computational intelligence: wavelet neural networks, hybrid wavelet neuro-fuzzy systems, identification, forecasting, clustering, diagnostics, fault detection in technical, economical, medical and ecological objects

Publications: She has more than 140 scientific publications, including 4 monographs. Publications Last 3 Years:

1. Bodyanskiy Ye., Vynokurova O. Hybrid adaptive wavelet-neuro-fuzzy system for chaotic time series identification//Information Sciences. – 2013. – 220. - P.170-179.
2. Bodyanskiy Ye., Dolotov A., Vynokurova O. Evolving spiking wavelet-neuro-fuzzy self-learning system//Applied Soft Computing. – 2014. – 14. – P. 252-258.
3. Bodyanskiy Ye., Vynokurova E.A., Dolotov A.I. Self-learning cascade spiking neural network for fuzzy clustering based on Group Method of Data Handling//J. of Automation and Information Sciences. – 2013. – 45. – №3. – P.23-33.
4. Bodyanskiy Ye., Pliss I., Vynokurova O. Flexible neo-fuzzy-neuron and neuro-fuzzy network for monitoring time-series properties//Sci. J.

of Riga Technical University: Information Technology and Management Science. – 2013. – 16. – P.47-52.
5. Bodyanskiy Ye., Kharchenko O., Vynokurova O. Least squares support vector machine based on wavelet-neuron//Sci. J. of Riga Technical University: Information Technology and Management Science. – 17. – 2014. – P. 19-24.
6. Bodyanskiy Ye., Peleshko D., Vynokurova O., Tatarinova Yu. Architecture of Hybrid Generalized Additive Neuro-Fuzzy System in Modelling Technological Process//Proc. XIII-th IEEE Int. Conf. "The Experience of Designing and Application of CAD Systems in Microelectronics." – Lviv-Polyana, Ukraine, 2015. – P. 333-335.
7. Vynokurova O., Pliss I., Peleshko D., Bodyanskiy Ye. Multilayer neuro-fuzzy system for solving on-line diagnostics tasks//Eds. by G. Setlak, K. Markov "Computational Models for Business and Engineering Domains." – Rzeszow-Sofia: ITHEA, 2014. – P. 52-59.
8. Bodyanskiy Ye., Pliss I.P., Tatarinova Yu., Vynokurova O. Hybrid Generalized Additive Type-2 Fuzzy-Wavelet-Neural Network in Dynamic Data Mining Tasks//Information Technology and Management Science. – 2015. – 18. - P. 70-77.
9. Bodyanskiy Ye., Pliss I., Setlak G., Vynokurova O. On-line Hybrid System of Computational Intelligence for Data Streams Adaptive Processing//Sensor and Transductors. – Spain: IFSA Publising, 2015. – 12. -195. - P. 62-68
10. Bodyanskiy Ye., Setlak G., Peleshko D., Vynokurova O. Hybrid Generalized Additive Neuro-Fuzzy System and its Adaptive Learning Algorithms//The 8th IEEE International Conference on Intelligent Data Acquisition and Advanced Computing Systems: Technology and Applications 24-26 September 2015, Warsaw, Poland. – P. 328-333

Iryna Pliss

Affiliation: Kharkiv National University of Radio Electronics

Education: In 1970 she graduated with honour from Kharkiv National University of Radio Electronics. In 1979 she defended the Ph.D. thesis. In 1983 she received an academic title of Senior Researcher.

Address: 14 Nauky av., Kharkiv, 61166, Ukraine

Research and Professional Experience: She is a Leading Researcher of the Control Systems Research Laboratory at Kharkiv National University of Radio Electronics.

Professional Appointments: hybrid systems of computational intelligence: adaptive, neuro-, fuzzy- real-time systems, including problems connected with control, identification, forecasting, clustering, diagnostics, fault detection in technical, economical, medical and ecological objects.

Publications: She has more than 160 scientific publications. Publications Last 3 Years:

1. Bodyanskiy Ye., Pliss I., Vynokurova O. Flexible neo-fuzzy-neuron and neuro-fuzzy network for monitoring time-series properties//Sci. J. of Riga Technical University: Information Technology and Management Science. – 2013. – 16. – P.47-52.
2. Vynokurova O., Pliss I., Peleshko D., Bodyanskiy Ye. Multilayer neuro-fuzzy system for solving on-line diagnostics tasks//Eds. by G. Setlak, K. Markov "Computational Models for Business and Engineering Domains." – Rzeszow-Sofia: ITHEA, 2014. – P. 52-59.
3. Bodyanskiy Ye., Boiko O.O., Pliss I.P. Adaptive method of hybrid learning for evolving neuro-fuzzy system//Cybernetics and Systems Analysis. – 2015. – Vol. 51. – №. 4. – P. 500-505.
4. Bodyanskiy Ye., Shafronenko A., Volkova V. Adaptive fuzzy probabilistic clustering of incomplete data//Int. J. "Information Models and Analyses." – 2013. – 2. - №2. – P.112-117.
5. Bodyanskiy Ye., Tyshchenko O., Pliss I. Reservoir forecasting neuro-fuzzy network and its learning//Int. J. "Information Theories and Applications." – 2013. – 20. - №3. – P.203-209.
6. Bodyanskiy Ye., Pliss I.P., Tatarinova Yu., Vynokurova O. Hybrid Generalized Additive Type-2 Fuzzy-Wavelet-Neural Network in Dynamic Data Mining Tasks//Information Technology and Management Science. – 2015. – 18. - P. 70-77.
7. Bodyanskiy Ye., Pliss I., Setlak G., Vynokurova O. On-line Hybrid System of Computational Intelligence for Data Streams Adaptive Processing//Sensor and Transductors. – Spain: IFSA Publising, 2015. – 12. -195. - P. 62-68

Pavlo Mulesa

Affiliation: Uzhhorod National University

Education: He graduated in mathematics from the Uzhhorod National University in 2005 and in 2015 received the degree of Ph.D.

Address: 3 Narodna Square, 88000, Uzhhorod, Ukraine. Phone: +38 03122 333–41, e-mail: ppmulesa@gmail.com.

Research and Professional Experience: He is vice-dean of mathematical faculty, associate professor of cybernetics and applied mathematics department at Uzhhorod National University.

Professional Appointments: artificial intelligence, neural networks, fuzzy systems, medical data mining.

Publications: He has more than 20 scientific publications.

INDEX

A

B

C

D

E

F

G

H

I

J

L

M

S

T

U

V

W